PELICAN BOOKS
A 202
THE MAGISTRATES' COURTS
F. T. GILES

The Magistrates' Courts

WHAT THEY DO · HOW THEY DO IT
AND WHY

F. T. GILES
LL. B.

PENGUIN BOOKS

Penguin Books Ltd, Harmondsworth, Middlesex
U.S.A.: Penguin Books Inc., 3300 Clipper Mill Road, Baltimore 11, Md
[*Educational Representative:*
D. C. Heath & Co, 285 Columbus Avenue, Boston 16, Mass]
CANADA: Penguin Books (Canada) Ltd, 47 Green Street,
Saint Lambert, Montreal, P.Q.
AUSTRALIA: Penguin Books Pty Ltd, 762 Whitehorse Road,
Mitcham, Victoria
SOUTH AFRICA: Penguin Books (S.A.) Pty Ltd, Gibraltar House,
Regents Road, Sea Point, Cape Town

—

Specially written for Pelican Books
and first published in 1949
Revised and reprinted 1951 and 1955

BY THE SAME AUTHOR

The Juvenile Courts, Their Work and Problems
Children in Trouble
The Criminal Law

Made and printed in Great Britain
by Hunt, Barnard & Co, Ltd,
Aylesbury

CONTENTS

CHAPTER 1

THE MAGISTRATES' REALM

WHAT place has the magistrates' court in the judicial scheme of things?

Many people dismiss it as 'where they do the drunks'.

This is about as true as to say that the Post Office is 'where they sell the stamps'.

The Post Office does sell stamps but it does a great deal more. Besides its manifold postal activities it is the maid of all work of the great Departments of State.

In like manner the magistrates' court is the Cinderella of the judicial system. 'It does everything,' it was once wittily said, 'which it would not pay a lawyer to do.'

There is enough truth and falsity in this generalization to make it worth consideration. Its truth is brought home to us when we realize that most of the litigants who come before the magistrates have no legal advisers because even in these days they cannot afford them. Its falsity will be realized when we remember that many solicitors have a remunerative magisterial court practice and many barristers including some of the most famous have appeared before the justices in their early days and often in the days of their success.

For though measured in terms of money and property the powers of magistrates are small and restricted, measured in terms of liberty and life they are broad and weighty. In many cases they can impose heavy penalties and sentences of imprisonment up to six months; in some, up to twelve; in a few up to two years. At the hands of a bench of magistrates sitting in a small town hall where to the uninitiated it would seem as if nothing more important was going forward than a meeting of the local council, a man found guilty of a serious crime may forfeit his freedom, his reputation, and his future just as certainly as before a 'red judge' in the brooding atmosphere of the Old Bailey.

The ruin which a conviction may bring upon an individual

in the highly organized society in which we live to-day is not dependent upon the status of the court which tries him or upon the degree of punishment imposed. It depends almost always upon the finding of guilt.

Let us see in outline what the powers of magistrates are.

First of all, the magistrates' court is the great clearing house of crime. All criminal prosecutions, with the rarest exceptions which it would be pedantry to notice here, begin in the magistrates' courts and nearly ninety-nine out of every hundred end there. According to the criminal statistics for 1952, the magistrates dealt with nearly 700,000 criminal charges great and small, whilst Assizes and Quarter Sessions dealt with only 22,000.

Until about a hundred years ago all the graver crimes could be tried only before a judge and jury. To-day the magistrates are empowered to deal with many of these offences from stealing upwards, so that we find that including charges against juveniles the summary courts dealt with 110,000 of these offences whilst only 22,153 went on for trial at the higher courts.

In other words, our criminal legal system has undergone a quiet, almost unnoticed and typically English revolution. The jury has left the jury box and taken its place upon the bench. The judge has stepped down to the clerk's seat to act as legal adviser to the layman.

In addition to criminal prosecutions, the magistrates have a great deal of what is termed 'civil work'. The difference between criminal and civil cases is fundamental and an attempt to explain it is made in Chapter 8.

The most important branch of this civil jurisdiction is the making of separation and maintenance orders upon the application of husbands and wives.

This work is very similar to that of the Divorce Division of the High Court of Justice. The legal problems that trouble the judges of that Court are often exactly like those which arise in the magistrates' courts. True the powers of the justices are not so great. They can only separate, where the judges can divorce. But the magistrates usually have to labour under difficulties unknown in the High Court. More often than not the parties come straight into court from the street. Their evidence has to be extracted there and then, whereas for the Divorce Court Judge it is carefully sifted in advance by solicitors who specialize in the work and is presented by experienced barristers.

Closely akin to these cases are applications under the Guardianship of Infants Act, 1925, and under the Adoption of Children Act, 1950. In the first the magistrates have to decide between the rival claims of parents. From the legal point of view the Act is interesting in that it allows the magistrates to take part in work which had hitherto been done exclusively in the Chancery Division of the High Court.

The first Adoption of Children Act was passed in 1926 and was an even greater innovation. Adoption, an important feature of Roman law, was unknown to English law. Until this Act was passed one person could not adopt another. Often sympathetic people would bring up a child until he was old enough to leave school and earn money, when the parents seeing in him a source of income would take him back, however disadvantageous it might be to the child and however distressing to his benefactors.

Under the Act the parents of such a child surrender their rights and obligations and the adopters assume them. The parents can never regain their status without the consent of the adopters.

This Act too throws an interesting light on the way our law is developing, for applications may be made either to the High Court, to the County Courts, or to the magistrates. Needless to say, most of the orders under the Act are made in the summary courts as they are by far the cheapest and handiest of these tribunals.

Other important branches of magisterial activity are the making or refusal of orders for the maintenance of illegitimate children; the granting or refusal of ejectment orders in small tenancies; licensing law; the enforcement of the payment of rates and debts due to certain privileged creditors such as Her Majesty's Commissioners of Income Tax, and gas, water, and electricity undertakings; and finally, a mass of miscellaneous business such as the granting of moneylenders' certificates and the making of statutory declarations.

So much then for a first cursory glance. Justices have been derided as the great unpaid. But, as it is hoped has been shown in this short chapter, they have a role of increasing importance to play in public life. That their work has professionally expanded since the days of Crécy is in itself proof that the justices in the main have done their work conscientiously and well.

Indeed so wide and varied are the powers of the magistrates that a sound knowledge of their work is as good a practical introduction to the understanding of our law as any. Assuredly such a study is worth while. To-day the law touches us at every point and nearly every question of outstanding public interest has some facet which a knowledge of legal principles and procedure will light up.

As for those who have to administer the law, in particular the lay magistrates, it should certainly be well worth their while to make an effort to acquire in outline at least some knowledge of the law they have the honour to take part in administering if only, to put it at its lowest, because it will be a protection for themselves. Besides being entrusted with powers and rights, the magistrate if he misuses them is subject to pains and penalties, as, for example, damages awarded against him in the High Court for locking up someone he ought not to have locked up. This does not often happen; but what comes all too frequently is polite but none the less distasteful criticism when a case dealt with in a summary court is unfavourably reviewed on appeal by the judges of the Queen's Bench.

It may be said, 'But the clerk is there to keep the magistrates right on the law'. Perfectly true, but the clerk will not pay the damages and criticism of the court's decision will touch him only indirectly. Furthermore in these days when judicial procedure is becoming ever more complicated and magisterial powers ever wider, the wisest clerk may miss the mark and no one can be regarded as infallible.

To carry out his duties intelligently, the magistrate ought at least to have some general knowledge of his position and powers. He is not an automaton or a rubber stamp. He has wide discretions which it is his duty to know how to use. He cannot do so if he is led along like a blind man by more learned or more dominant colleagues because he lacks the knowledge which would enable him to understand what is being done for himself.

Moreover, the study of the law is its own reward. There is artistry in the lawyer's craft from which the student can reap pleasure and profit as from the study of any other art. Great judgements and great laws are comparable to great paintings and great music. The judgement of Solomon has stirred the imagination of every generation since it was delivered. Magna Carta, Habeas Corpus, the Declaration of Rights move us as surely and as deeply as the 'Marseillaise' and 'God save the Queen'.

Most people look upon the law as an odd collection of rules and regulations arbitrarily framed and capriciously enforced without rhyme or reason. Slight acquaintance reveals some show of reason but little rhyme. But closer intimacy discovers in its records the majestic trend of man's efforts to achieve justice, freedom, and equality. A tendency to prosiness upon occasion must be conceded, but this is heavily offset by the many brilliant expositions and arguments to be found in our law books which are a delight to read and a stimulus to follow.

CHAPTER 2

ACTS OF PARLIAMENT

HAVING made this brief and superficial survey of magisterial jurisdiction, let us now spend an hour in a law library.

Round us, shelf upon shelf, we see books about law. You ask in dismay 'Where can I begin?'

The answer is 'Obviously with Acts of Parliament'.

Acts of Parliament are the foundation of the magistrates' powers. Take everything else away and they would still have plenty of authority to exercise. Without them they would have very little.

We shall find the Acts on a convenient shelf bound up in annual volumes with an index at the end. Let us take down the volume for 1952. Looking through the pages we shall see many Acts which can have little appeal for the magisterial reading public. 'Diplomatic Immunities (Commonwealth Countries and Republic of Ireland) Act' – 'Prisons (Scotland) Act', – 'Miners Welfare Act' – these are the page headings that meet the eye.

But if we look at Chapter 55 – each Act is a separate chapter numbered in the order in which it came into force in its year of enactment – we shall find the Magistrates' Courts Act, 1952.

The Act is a difficult one to read, but even to those who have never looked at an Act of Parliament before it is clearly something to do with magistrates and their courts. And indeed it is the Act upon which almost all present-day magisterial procedure is based.

An act like this is sometimes called 'procedural'; that is, one of a species of Acts which tell courts and magistrates and judges how they should try cases, how they should run their courts, and what powers they have to carry out their decisions.

Another and much larger group of Acts create offences such as stealing and drunkenness, or permit one person to complain of the behaviour of another, as for example to bring a petition for divorce or to make an application for a separation order.

Let us take down another volume and look at an Act of this kind. In the volume for 1930 we shall find that Chapter 43 is the famous Road Traffic Act of that year. In this we shall discover many actions which are made criminal offences but nothing about how those offences are to be tried.

Thus Section 12 (1) says that 'If any person drives a motor vehicle on a road without due care and attention or without reasonable consideration for other persons using the road he shall be guilty of an offence'. But the section does not say who is to try the offence nor what procedure is to be followed.

If, however, we turn to Section 113 (1) we shall find this – 'Save as otherwise expressly provided, all offences under this Act shall be prosecuted under the Summary Jurisdiction Acts'. That is to say, the Magistrates' Courts Act which has now replaced the Summary Jurisdiction Acts is tacked on to the Road Traffic Act. Instead of setting out in each separate statute how offences are to be tried under it, Parliament simply says, 'Deal with these offences as I have told you to deal with offences generally under the Magistrates' Courts Act'. 'Procedural Acts' are therefore a kind of legislative labour-saving device. Just as one balance can be used to weigh all sorts of goods, so is the Magistrates' Courts Act used to try all sorts of offences and complaints.

Many Acts, especially modern ones, do not attempt to set out everything which the legislature hopes to make unlawful by means of them. They empower a Minister or the Privy Council to make regulations or orders. When these are properly sanctioned they have all the force of the Act of Parliament under which they are made.

Thus, turning back to the Road Traffic Act, we shall find that the Act itself creates a number of offences – as, for example, reckless or dangerous driving, Section 11; careless driving, Section 12; driving under the influence of drink or drugs, Section 15. But in addition to this we shall find if we turn to Section 111 that the Minister of Transport has the power to make regulations the infringement of which is also an offence triable in the summary courts in the same way as other offences enacted by the Act itself.

In this way the scope of the Act has been greatly enlarged. Indeed far more offences have been created by regulations than by the Road Traffic Acts themselves – obstruction by motor-cars, non-compliance with traffic signs, failure to keep a motor vehicle in roadworthy trim are all to be found in the regulations and not in one of the Acts.

Like the Acts of Parliament from which they depend, regulations and orders are bound up in annual volumes. One series of them should be found at every court, though it is to be feared that at many they are not.

More often than not Acts of Parliament do not stand alone. Frequently two Acts have to be read together; sometimes several Acts have to be consulted. A later Act may add to an earlier or modify it or attempt to clarify its meaning. The Road Traffic Act, 1934, for example, followed the Road Traffic Act, 1930. Section 6 of the earlier Act authorized magistrates to endorse the licence of a motorist convicted of any criminal offence in connexion with the driving of a motor vehicle. It gave them unfettered discretion whether to endorse or not. But Section 5 of the later Act put a limit upon this discretion. It provided that whenever a motorist is convicted of exceeding the speed limit his licence *must* be endorsed unless there are special reasons for the court to order otherwise.

Acts which are so intimately linked as these are often put together in one bundle and given one title. Thus the two Road Traffic Acts instead of being spoken of separately are entitled 'the Road Traffic Acts'.

In reading an Act of Parliament we must not take it for granted that the words it contains are always used as we use them in everyday speech. When, for example, the man in the street talks about 'land' he usually means ground which has not been built upon. But 'land' in most Acts of Parliament dealing with property has a much wider meaning than this. It means not only the land itself but any buildings upon it, minerals beneath it, crops growing in its soil, trees and hedges, and even rights of way across it.

How shall we know if a particular Act contains words which must be read in a special way? Most Acts of any length contain what is called a 'definition section'. Usually it is at the end of the statute. Here we shall find those words to which the legislature requires the courts to attach a particular meaning.

Let us see how such a section helps. A man is summoned under the Road Traffic Acts for being the owner of a car and allowing it to be used without efficient brakes. 'But I am not the owner,' he tells the court, and produces a hire-purchase agreement which distinctly says that until all the instalments have been paid he will not be the owner. If we turn to the definition section of the Road Traffic Act, 1930, Section 121, we shall find 'Owner' defined as 'including the person in possession of the vehicle under a hire-purchase agreement'.

General rules of interpretation are assembled in the Interpretation Act, 1889. In Acts of Parliament passed after 1850, masculine words shall include feminine, words in the singular shall include the plural, words in the plural include the singular, unless of course a contrary intention appears. The word 'person' in an Act includes a body corporate such as a limited company or public corporation, again 'unless the contrary intention appears'. The Act also gives a great number of definitions, from 'month' to 'court of summary jurisdiction'.

The subject of interpretation is far too large to be dealt with here in any detail, but one final word of warning may be of value. Parliamentary draughtsmen are disarmingly polite. They often write 'may' when they mean 'must'. If an Act tells a bench that they 'may' do something, it usually means that they must though quite likely they would rather not. Thus, if a rate collector proves that a ratepayer has not paid his rates, the Distress for Rates Act, 1849, tells the magistrates that they 'may' issue a warrant of distress to recover what is due. This 'may' means 'must'. So too generally do the phrases 'it shall be lawful', – 'if the Justices think fit' – 'may cause'. The general rule is that if a court is empowered to do something and is legitimately asked to do so, then it must comply.

CHAPTER 3

CASES

YOU may now think that with Acts of Parliament and regulations to tell magistrates what they may do and how they may do it, nothing more remains but to go into court and set to work.

Some legal systems do stop short at this point and leave their judges and magistrates to their own devices. The English system does not. Part of it – a very important part – is what is known as 'case law', that is to say law formed from actual cases which have come into the courts for decision.

We can best see how it works if we take an actual illustration.

White comes before a bench summoned for obstructing the road with his motor-car. In his defence he says, 'I didn't obstruct the road. I left it on the pavement'. This court retorts, 'The word "road" includes pavement as well as the carriage way', and convicts White.

Black comes before the bench in the next town summoned for an exactly similar offence. He raises the same point. The magistrates here think he is right. 'Road' they hold means only that part of the highway used by vehicles, and Black is acquitted.

Thus it happens that acting under a very well-known regulation of a very well-known Act of Parliament two neighbouring towns have a completely different law on this point of leaving motor-cars on footways.

Or rather they might have had up to 1932. For in 1932 the 'pavementeers' met their Waterloo. One was acquitted by a summary court and the police appealed to the Judges of the High Court. The Judges decided that the word 'road' as used in the Road Traffic Act, 1930, includes the footway as well as the carriage-way, and henceforth not only White's bench will so regard the pavement but also the bench in the neighbouring town which acquitted Black, and all other benches throughout the country.

In coming to this decision the judges have added an item of law which was not authoritatively established before. A record of the proceedings was made and has now become a 'case' treasured up for the future guidance of the courts in a number of collections of cases. The police officer in the case was called Bryant and the defendant Marx. Hence the case goes into the judicial records labelled *Bryant* v. *Marx*, followed by these mysterious figures (1932), 96 J.P. 383. 1932, of course, was the year the case was decided; the letters J.P. indicate that it is to be found in the collection of cases published by the periodical called the *Justice of the Peace*, volume 96, page 383.

Bryant v. *Marx* shows the English case law system at its best. Here was a simple point frequently cropping up which one court was deciding in one way and another in the opposite way. There was one law for Black and another for White. From 1932 onwards Black and White must be treated alike. *Bryant* v. *Marx* is clear, unambiguous and authoritative. It is 'fair as a star' as Wordsworth wrote 'when only one is shining in the sky'.

But like stars, cases are more often found in constellations than alone, giving more light but less guidance. Instead of one decision dealing with one point, as in the case of *Bryant* v. *Marx*, we shall sometimes find a dozen, and the question is which one should we follow.

For example, The Employers and Workmen Act, 1875, gives magistrates certain powers to compensate workmen who have been wrongfully dismissed. Immediately arises the question 'Who is a workman?' Nearly a score of cases have been decided upon the point. Tailors and shoemakers it has been held are workmen. Barbers, telegraph clerks, and grocers' assistants are not. Neither are bus conductors nor bus drivers; but if he is expected to do running repairs to his vehicle, then the bus driver is a 'workman'.

In a multitude of counsellors whom should we follow?

If there is no case fairly like the one the magistrates have to decide they must try to find an underlying principle which has guided the judges in their decisions, and apply that principle to their particular case. Sometimes they will be so fortunate as to find a case in which the judges have formulated a principle themselves. In these 'workmen' cases, for instance, is one called *Cook* v. *North Metropolitan Tramways Company* (1887), 51 J.P. 630, where one of the judges drew a distinction between 'manual labour' and 'manual work'.

'I think,' said Mr Justice Grantham, 'a fairly satisfactory distinction may be drawn between those whose labour is continuous and requires no application of thought and those whose labour requires the application of a certain amount of thought and skill.'

That is to say, he limited the meaning of the word 'workman' in the Employers and Workmen Act, 1875, to those engaged in the lower forms of labour. Those engaged in the higher forms demanding greater skill and thought must take their complaints to the less accessible and generally more expensive County Courts.

What is the effect of these cases and others like them (for there are many thousands of them)? Firstly, each one makes the law a little more uniform. Secondly, each makes the law a little more complex. We have another point to remember and we can never be quite sure if we have 'remembered' – as the euphemistic phrase goes – all the cases bearing on a particular point; or, if there are some which do not seem to agree, whether we have picked out the right one.

Take down a volume of cases. Most of those which began in the summary courts make extremely entertaining reading. Every phase of human activity comes up for review, from the vagaries of homing pigeons to the difficulties of baking loaves so that they go over the counter an integral number of pounds in weight. Quite an interesting parlour game is to guess on which side the judges will come down and then to read the reasons they gave for their decisions.

The judgements in these cases are not unlike a sermon. The clergyman takes a phrase or a verse from the Scriptures and discusses it. The judges take a phrase or a word from the law and explain it. There are differences of course. The minister can take his text from anywhere he likes according to what he regards as the most pressing spiritual need of his congregation at the moment. The judges have no such latitude. They can deal only with the point of law they are asked to examine – in the cases we have discussed, for example, whether 'road' includes 'pavement' or whether a particular occupation comes within the Employers and Workmen Act, 1875.

But whilst we need take not the slightest notice of what the priest tells us, the magistrates must conform with the decisions of the judges whether they think it right or not. This is what is known as the 'binding effect' of case law – all lower courts are bound by the decisions of the judges of the High Court and the appeal courts above them.

But this is not to say that a decision of the judges stands for all time. The case of *Bryant* v. *Marx* was decided by a 'Divisional Court' of three judges of the High Court. Most of the cases which affect magisterial court work are decided in this court. Superior to it are the Court of Appeal and the Court of Criminal Appeal. Above them in turn is the House of Lords. At some time in the future the Court of Appeal or the Court of Criminal Appeal may express disagreement with *Bryant* v. *Marx*. From that moment it will have lost its potency and the decision of the higher court will take its place. Later possibly the question may be considered by the House of Lords. The law lords may think *Bryant* v. *Marx* was after all right, in which event we shall have come full circle and the rule it laid down will be re-established.

The great destroyer of case law, however, is the legislature. Not even a decision of the House of Lords is proof against an Act of Parliament. If to-morrow Parliament decreed that 'road' does not include 'pavement' *Bryant* v. *Marx* would be dead without hope of resurrection.

One day Parliament may decide to replace the Employers and Workmen Act, 1875, with a more up-to-date measure. It may decide that all such complaints shall in future be decided in the County Courts or conversely that all workmen, skilled and unskilled, may bring their disputes to the magistrates. Whatever happens we may be sure that the tangle of workmen's cases with their finely-spun distinctions and heavily laboured differences will disappear into the limbo of 'old, unhappy, far-off things and battles long ago'.

How do these cases arise? They are all decisions of the Judges of the Supreme Court, sometimes of a judge deciding a case for the first time it has come before a court, but more often of judges who are reviewing the decision of a lower court from which one of the parties has appealed.

All are concerned with a problem of law, not a problem of fact. In *Bryant* v. *Marx*, for example, there was no dispute about the facts. Mr Marx did not dispute what the police said. He admitted that he had left his car on the pavement. But he claimed that the law did not extend to pavements.

Similarly in the workmen cases, the question was not whether in fact a man had been employed in a particular capacity – as a motor driver, a tailor, a shoemaker – but whether, admitting that he had, was he then a 'workman' within the meaning of the Act.

It is important to keep this distinction between law and fact clear. In every case, no matter in what court it is heard, one side is saying to the judges or the magistrates – 'These are the facts. Now administer the law'. Usually the other side if it is contesting the case replies – 'These are not the facts. We dispute them', in which case the suit resolves itself into a battle upon the facts. Less often we hear the reply, 'We admit the facts but we deny that they bring us within the law'.

This was the reply given in *Bryant* v. *Marx*. The magistrate thought it was the correct contention and he upheld it. The police were dissatisfied and appealed to the judges of the Divisional Court. They upheld the view of the police. The decision was carefully recorded in the law reports and so it took its place as part of our law of obstruction with the Act and regulation which create the offence.

CHAPTER 4

'STONE'

I⊤ may be that in our search for law books we shall not find any volumes of cases. Possibly too diligent search will fail to reveal a single regulation or order; not even a series of the Acts of Parliament. If this be so, our case is desperate but not hopeless. For assuredly there will be *Stone*.

What the sun is to the British Empire so is *Stone* to the magistrates' courts. Without it a court never sits. Someone is bound to have a copy – usually there is one in the local library. Get hold of that copy and spend a quiet half hour with it. Your time will be put to good use.

It is a blue volume* entitled in gilt *Stone's Justices' Manual*. Externally it is as like Sir John Falstaff as a book can be. But there the resemblance ends. Internally it is a work of high courage and industry. The title 'Manual' is apt – something ready to our hand in a moment of difficulty. But it is more than a manual – it is a monument – a monument to the craft of the bookbinder and to the ingenuity of its editor. In each annual volume place has to be found for the year's harvest of statutes and regulations and of cases affecting magisterial procedure; whilst at the same time Acts of Parliament which have been repealed during the year and cases which have become obsolete have to be taken out – in all, a feat of digestion and elimination to test the stoutest constitution.

Stone is used in two ways, properly and improperly. Let us dispose of the improper first. *Stone* is a general practitioner to whom we can turn for guidance and information upon general problems arising in the course of a sitting. But he is not a specialist, and when some unusual or difficult point of law is raised, it is not fair to expect to find within

*Owing to bookbinding difficulties, *Stone* now appears in two volumes, but the publishers hope to revert to the single volume as soon as possible.

his covers, bursting though they are with erudition, as full and as exhaustive an examination of the problem as another work which specializes in the particular branch of the law concerned is able to devote to it.

In all such cases we should pass on from *Stone* to the Acts of Parliament and the cases which affect the question before making our decision. No one volume can hope to provide us with details which fill many. The best it can do is to supply a careful summary which will put us on the track of the specialists. This *Stone* can certainly claim to do.

We shall get most out of the book if we take the trouble to study how it is put together and to see how it is intended to be used. The volume consists of five parts and an appendix. Part I is devoted to matters about the Court and the Clerk. Some of the more important of these questions are dealt with in Chapters 5 and 6 of this book.

Part II deals with magistrates' courts generally. Part III deals with questions of practice and procedure; whilst Part IV is divided up into chapters dealing with the various branches of law the magistrates have to administer. These chapters are arranged alphabetically and one way of looking up a point quickly is to turn at once to the appropriate chapter. Thus, under 'Dogs' we shall find the Act of Parliament and cases dealing with dog licences, dog collars, dangerous dogs and so on; under 'Shops', the Acts and regulations relating to early closing and the hours of shop assistants.

But we must not expect a chapter for everything we can think of. If we fail to find a chapter under the first title which occurs to us we must try to find what we want under another. There is, for instance, no chapter entitled 'Stealing'. This will be found included under the more general heading 'Larceny'. There is no chapter headed 'Murder'. This comes under 'Person (Offences against the)'. But after a little practice we shall astonish our uninitiated colleagues at the dexterity with which we are able to turn things up thanks to the alphabetical arrangement of the work.

Now let us make another practical experiment in finding our way about the book. Suppose a pavement problem similar to the one to which we referred in Chapter 3 has arisen. We can hardly expect to find a chapter headed 'Pavement' or 'Footway'. The point is undoubtedly buried in the mass of motor legislation all included under the general heading 'Road Traffic'. We cannot search through this at short notice, so in such a case we turn to the compendious index at the end of the volume. Under 'motor vehicles' and against the sub-heading 'obstruction' is the number of a page upon which we shall find the 'Motor Vehicles (Construction and Use) Regulations'. One of them – Paragraph 88 – is the regulation which prohibits obstruction. It reads 'No person in charge of a motor vehicle shall cause the motor vehicle to stand on a road so as to cause any unnecessary obstruction thereof'.

At the foot of the page is a note 'x' which refers us to the case we have already noticed in Chapter 3 (*Bryant* v. *Marx*) with the terse summary 'Road includes footway'.

So far Dr Stone has stood us in good stead. But we ought not to be content to leave matters here. In his footnote he has suggested a specialist and told us where we can find him. We ought to turn to a report of *Bryant* v. *Marx* and see how nearly it falls in with the facts of our own case. The worthy doctor having helped us to a correct diagnosis we ought to consult the specialist before finally making our decision.

There are two other indexes in the volume which are worth noting.

Towards the beginning you will find a 'Table of Statutes' in chronological order. If you are looking for an Act of Parliament and happen to know the year it became law you will be able to find where it appears in the book with the help of this index.

It is followed by a 'Table of cases cited in the work'. Amongst them in alphabetical order we shall find the two cases quoted in the last chapter. The list contains some eight to nine thousand, and these are but a fraction of all the decided cases in English law and indeed are but a selection of all those affecting the magistrates and their work.

The date following the name of each case is, as we have seen, the year in which the case was reported, and then follow those cryptic letters and figures about which something has already been said in Chapter 3.

They tell us where we may find reports of these cases. Law reports are published by a number of different houses. As we saw in Chapter 3, one series is issued by the weekly periodical, the *Justice of the Peace*. Some are published by newspapers, as for example *The Times Law Reports* indicated by the letters 'T.L.R.'. Some confine themselves to the activities of a particular court, as, for example, the *Reports of the Court of Criminal Appeal*, indicated by the letters Cr. App. R. A list of the abbreviations used is given in *Stone* a few pages in front of the 'Table of Statutes'.

Pride of place is given in these citations to the *Law Reports* which are regarded as quasi-official because the judges take some part in their compilation. Where a case is reported in the *Law Reports* we shall find the year of publication in square brackets thus – [1930] – instead of round – (1930) – followed by letters which show in which branch of the Supreme Court the case was decided – Q.B. for Queen's Bench; A.C. for Appeals to the Judicial Committee of the Privy Council and the House of Lords; P. for the Probate, Divorce and Admiralty Division; and C. for Chancery.

Let us conclude with a practical illustration of the system of citation. A case is cited as follows – *Black* v. *White*, [1929] 2 K.B. 184; 93 J.P. 68; 45 T.L.R. 101.

This means that we shall find the case in the second volume of the *Law Reports* for the King's Bench Division at page 184; or in volume 93 of the *Justice of the Peace Reports* at page 68; or in the forty-fifth volume of *The Times Law Reports* at page 101.

You may ask, 'Why give all these different citations?' Because as we have already hinted law libraries are not always as complete as we might wish them to be. Usually one library will have one series of cases. Not many will have two. Few indeed three. As our worthy family practitioner the venerable *Stone* cannot know which series we have and which we have not, he gives as many citations as he can in the hope that we shall possess one of them.

CHAPTER 5

SOME PRELIMINARY QUESTIONS

BEFORE taking his seat a Justice must take the oath of allegiance and the judicial oath. A county Justice may do this before his fellow Justices in open court at a Quarter Sessions of the county. A Justice for a borough may take the oath before the mayor or any two Justices or two Councillors for the borough.

The terms of the oath are worth longer and more careful thought than most oaths are given.

'... I will do right to all manner of people after the laws and usages of the realm without fear or favour, affection or ill-will.'

The words are a reminder that magistrates like all others entrusted with judicial powers are the ministers and servants of the Law and not its critics. Yet it is not uncommon to find a justice making a virtue of flouting some Act of which he does not approve or following some procedure of his own devising, comfortable in the knowledge that his hardihood is not likely to be challenged on appeal. Pet aversions popular at the moment are multiple stores, and Shops and Factories Act prosecutions. Vaccination whimsies had a great vogue at one time, but they are not what they were.

The next question is 'At what courts can a magistrate sit?' If he is appointed for a borough he can sit at any general summary court held in that borough. There is a growing tendency to specialize in some of the work so that only selected magistrates sit in the juvenile and matrimonial courts and as Licensing Justices.

Counties are divided into divisions and each magistrate is allocated to one of these divisions. He is competent to sit in any division, and there have been instances in the past where justices from one division have invaded another when a case in which they had a particular interest was being tried. Needless to say it is in just such cases that this rule of allocation should be most scrupulously observed. A justice who breaks so sensible a rule must at once arouse suspicions of his impartiality.

The number of justices who may sit to deal with a case is now determined by the Justices of the Peace (Size and Chairmanship of Bench) Rules, 1950. Rule 1 (2) provides that 'the number of county or borough justices sitting to deal with a case as a magistrates' court shall not be greater than seven'. In a letter of 30 November 1950, the Lord Chancellor intimated that 'although seven has been fixed as the maximum number of Justices to deal with a case', he was of opinion that 'only in exceptional circumstances should more than five Justices sit on a Petty Sessional Bench at the same time'.

The justices who hear a case have each one vote in deciding it. If the bench is equally divided, the proceedings may be heard afresh by a differently constituted court. If the justices do not agree to this the case must be dismissed. The chairman has no casting vote in the event of a tie but deadlock is sometimes avoided if a justice on one side or the other withdraws.

There are a few charges upon which one justice can adjudicate alone. For example he can deal with drunks and vagrants. But his powers are so limited that this rarely happens.

The above rules also provide for the annual election by the justices of each Petty Sessions of a chairman and one or more deputy chairmen. The election is by secret ballot.

Magistrates sometimes feel overshadowed by a too dominant chairman. It is, of course, desirable that witnesses and defendants should not be confused by a bombardment of questions directed at them from all along the bench, especially if several justices are sitting. But where a magistrate feels after the usual points have been elicited that it might be helpful to ask a question or two on a relevant matter there can be no objection to his doing so.

A much more serious complaint is that the Chairman

'does everything', deciding to acquit or convict and what sentence to impose in that event without a 'by your leave' to his colleagues. Usually a hint corrects this conduct. A magistrate may be prepared to tolerate it where he agrees with the decision. But it would be wrong for him to allow it to pass unchallenged if he did not agree. It is his duty to make known his views to his colleagues and if necessary to ask them to discuss the matter in the magistrates' private room.

Then there is the Clerk. He is the magistrates' legal adviser. Generally they will accept his ruling upon the law, but they are not bound to do so. They may prefer to accept and act upon the view put forward by one of the parties or his advocate. The responsibility for all the decisions of the Court is the Justices' not the Clerk's. Usually the Clerk has won the confidence of his bench and no questions of this kind arise, but it is well to be clear upon the relationship of one to the other. And just as the bench should heed carefully whatever the Clerk considers it right to point out to them and take a course opposed to his opinion only with hesitation and reluctance, so he should be ready to produce authorities in support of his arguments if asked for them and not to take umbrage if his advice is not followed.

As the magistrates bear the responsibility, it is only fair that as far as possible they should know what they are doing. To a Clerk who airily assured a magistrate he had asked to sign a number of mysterious documents that 'they were all right', the magistrate retorted 'Mr Clerk, I must know myself they are all right. My signature is going on the foot of them – not yours.'

Mr Clerk very likely knows a great deal more law than his magistrates do. He no doubt has much more experience than they. But this does not alter the fact that it is they and not he who have been chosen to be judges of their fellow citizens. Their relationship with him is very like that of a Cabinet Minister and the civil servant at the head of a Department of State. A prudent statesman will listen to any

advice his secretary may tender him, but the right and responsibility of decision is the minister's and not the civil
servant's.

The common tendency is for the Clerk because of his
constant preoccupation with legal forms and procedure to
be too regardful of the letter of the law, and for magistrates
impatient of restraints they do not understand to ride
roughshod over them in fulfilling what they consider to be
the spirit of the law. 'An ancient Clerk,' wrote Bacon,
'skilful in precedents, wary in proceeding, and understanding in the business of the Court, is an excellent finger of a
Court, and doth many times point the way to the Judge himself.' The 'excellent finger' having pointed out the way and
the dangers of straying from it, it will be for the magistrates
to choose whether they will take the risks inherent in such a
course. Occasions will arise when taking their courage in both
hands they will elect to do so. They will say to the Clerk, as
Sir Edward Hawke said to the master of the *Royal George*
amidst the reefs and currents and storm of Quiberon Bay –
'You have done your duty, Sir, in showing the danger; you
are now to obey my order and lay me alongside the *Soleil
Royal*.'

Of course, if the Clerk is ancient *de facto* as well as *de jure*
it will be kinder to use less colourful language. An indulgent
bench may think it better not to mention the *Soleil Royal*.

This brings us to a wider question still – the relationship
between bench and litigants. The magistrates have been
given powers to exercise in their discretion – to impose fines,
to inflict imprisonment, to enforce the payment of debts, to
make orders and to compel their observance. One side
comes before them to ask them to use those powers; the
other side to refrain. They know the law as we all do. The
law pays us all this pretty compliment so that we do not
escape it on the facile plea of ignorance. But the magistrates
cannot always be expected to know exactly upon what
authority a petitioner is asking them to act. If they call for
this information it is his business to supply it and to satisfy

them that he is right in thinking he is entitled to relief just as it is the business of the other party to the proceedings to try to show them that the exercise of such powers against him would be wrong.

The judges are constantly asking for assurances that they possess the powers and the authority one side is asking them to employ against the other. If we read verbatim reports of the cases they have tried we shall find them constantly interrupting counsel in the course of their argument with 'Why do you say that, Mr – ?' – 'On what authority do you base that contention?' The magistrates will do well to make the learned Judges their model. If they have no hesitation in asking for information and accepting instruction assuredly neither need the magistrates.

Finally a word about court manners. At first we may think everyone excessively polite, even fulsome. The moment a magistrate takes his seat upon the bench he becomes the 'learned magistrate' though possibly he may not yet have opened a law book. The Clerk is the 'learned Clerk'. Solicitors and counsel, 'learned solicitors and counsel'. Objections are made 'with great respect'. Criticism is prefaced by a tribute to the 'fairness with which my learned friend is conducting his case'. And so on.

Before we condemn such protestations as hypocritical let us remember that often in courts of law feeling runs high. Parties come into them to fight. Fighting develops heat; heat, indecorum; and indecorum may disturb, possibly wreck, that judicial detachment which it must be the courts' first object to preserve.

Just as we reduce friction in the internal combustion engine by generous supplies of oil, so we keep the court atmosphere down to a tolerable degree by the plentiful use of those civilities which to the newcomer may seem excessive.

CHAPTER 6

BIAS

ANOTHER group of questions which give justices a good deal of anxiety may be summed up in the question 'Ought I to sit?'

Clearly no judge in whatever court he may act ought to take part in a trial where his impartiality may be fairly questioned. The law leaves a great deal to the discretion of magistrates themselves. It is undesirable for example for a justice who has taken a prominent interest in animal welfare to adjudicate upon charges of cruelty to animals, but it is legally permissible for him to do so if he insists.

So too proceedings will not be invalidated even if one of the magistrates taking part is acquainted with or is even a friend of one of the parties. In small towns the magistrates are bound to be personally acquainted with many of the parties who appear before them and often they may be on the friendliest terms. If this alone could be treated as a valid objection it would frequently be very difficult to make up a bench of magistrates to whom no such objection could be taken.

But where the interest of a justice goes beyond that of the normal friendlily disposed fellow townsman, or where he already knows something of the facts of a dispute to be tried or at any rate may reasonably be thought to know something about them, he should then refuse to take part in the proceedings.

The position is well illustrated by a case which was decided in 1939 by the judges of the Divorce Division upon an appeal from a magistrates' court which had dealt with a matrimonial case (*Cottle* v. *Cottle* [1939], all E.R. 535). Before the hearing began the husband objected to the chairman of the magistrates taking part in the hearing because he was a friend of his wife's mother. The chairman overruled the objection characterizing it as frivolous.

The judges did not share this view and ordered the justices to hear the case again by a bench on which the magistrate to whom objection had been taken should not sit.

One judge who heard the appeal said 'I attach, as everybody must attach, the greatest importance to the fact that every litigant in a British court of justice should be satisfied that he is having an absolutely impartial trial and that there should be no suspicion of any undue influence.'

The President, whilst agreeing with this view, pointed out that it would be preposterous to hold that the mere fact of some sort of acquaintance existing between the parties would suggest bias. 'If we were to put such an exacting test upon the right of justices to sit,' he observed, 'it might very well be that the whole structure of summary jurisdiction might be upset. The whole essence of the local administration of justice and the great value of the functions of justice are that they do administer justice amongst people with whom they are acquainted, and of whose lives and family history they know something.'

In some cases the law strictly prohibits magistrates who hold certain positions or interests from sitting. Thus brewers and licensees if their businesses lie within their jurisdiction or an adjoining one must not take part in proceedings under the Licensing Acts, though they may try simple charges of drunkenness. Factory owners and trade union officials are similarly disqualified when proceedings are taken with respect to a factory with which they are associated.

Apart from these specific prohibitions, a decision may be upset if it can be shown that one of the justices had a financial interest in one of the parties or that he had taken some part in the proceedings from which it may reasonably be inferred that he would favour one side to the prejudice of the other.

The smallest financial interest will be sufficient to upset a decision – a few shares in a railway company when prosecuting someone for travelling on the railway without paying his fare, for instance. But if a magistrate who has a financial interest of this kind informs the parties of it and they then consent to his remaining to hear the case, it is highly improbable that the decision will be quashed on appeal.

Again, as for the financial interest, the 'challenge to the favour' can be met in any case of doubt if the magistrate frankly informs the parties of his position. If then they make no objection they cannot later raise the question on appeal, nor indeed can they do so if they or their advocates knew of the objection and did not themselves raise it at the opening of the proceedings before the magistrates.

Instances of decisions which have been challenged on the ground of 'favour' often occurred where magistrates were also councillors for a local authority and adjudicated upon proceedings instituted by the authority.

Such cases should never arise now since the passing of the Justices of the Peace Act, 1949, Section 3 of which provides that 'a justice of the peace who is a member of a local authority shall not act as a member of a court of quarter sessions or of a magistrates' court in any proceedings brought by or against, or by way of appeal from a decision of the authority or any committee or officer of the authority.'

In all these cases the safe rule is for any magistrate to withdraw if he is in any doubt or if he feels that reasonable people not interested in the proceedings might feel dubious of his impartiality. Lord Hewart put it well when in dealing with one of these questions he said 'Justice should not only be done, but be manifestly and undoubtedly seen to be done.'

Finally, if a magistrate does decide to withdraw, he should do so in a way which can leave no one in any doubt that he is taking no part in the hearing. He should not be content to remain upon the bench ostentatiously doing nothing. He should go and sit in the public part of the court house; or, better still, leave it altogether.

But this question – 'Ought I to sit?' may arise in other and more sinister ways. A magistrate will be invited to sit at an unusual hour or in an unusual place or to make one of an unusual bench. Whenever he is given such an invitation, he should make very sure that he is not being asked to take part in some dubious enterprise which may at best give rise to some local scandal and at worst be the subject of an appeal or special enquiry.

Very often these anomalous proceedings are perfectly legal so that neither of the parties has any grounds on which they can appeal to a higher court, but to-day this is no safeguard, since the invention of what is known as a special enquiry, which the Home Secretary or Lord Chancellor may order and which is usually presided over by some eminent judge.

Two of these enquiries have been held within recent years and both are good examples of the pitfalls which beset the unwary and inexperienced magistrate.

In the first of these cases, a man was charged with indecent assault. He should have appeared at the court which sat at 10 a.m. The Clerk of the Court arranged for him to appear at 9 a.m., and he was dealt with by magistrates who would not normally have sat at all on that day. Neither the police nor any representative for the prosecution were given an opportunity to be present at the hearing.

Obviously such proceedings were as wrong as they could be, and Lord Goddard who held the enquiry said of the justices who lent themselves to such practices that 'they did not recognize what must have been plain to any man of ordinary intelligence'. 'It is impossible,' he went on, 'to have confidence in their capacity to act as justices seeing that they did not recognize plain irregularities and had not the resolution to demand full and proper explanation from their Clerk.'

The second enquiry was held by Lord Justice Tucker in Yorkshire. The chairman of a local bench wanted to eject an employee from one of his cottages pursuant to the Small Tenements Recovery Act, 1838, and ordered the Clerk to summon a special Court for this purpose. The Court sat not in the usual court room but in the office of the Clerk and an order of ejectment was made.

Lord Justice Tucker condemned the proceedings in no uncertain terms. 'I acquit the chairman without doubt,' he wrote, 'of any intentional wrongdoing and I am satisfied that he never in any way discussed the merits of his case with the magistrates who heard the case, but the fact remains that he deliberately caused a special court to be summoned purely for his convenience. The only urgency in his case was that it was very inconvenient to him being without a groom. In my view, a magistrate, so far from using his position to further his own private convenience, should be prepared to put up with a greater degree of inconvenience than an ordinary litigant if there is any danger of conflict between his rights as an ordinary citizen and his position as a Justice of the Peace.

'Having decided to proceed before his own bench it was incumbent upon him to ensure that his case was dealt with in the normal and ordinary course with the usual degree of publicity, and to be careful to do nothing which could give any appearance of obtaining preferential treatment or taking part in the selection of the justices. Instead he caused a special court to be summoned in the occasional court house for his personal convenience and then invited a justice to sit and took him with him to the court because he feared one of the justices summoned might be adverse to him. Nothing can justify or excuse the chairman, who was for that afternoon an ordinary litigant, using his position as chairman to select a justice to try his own case and taking him with him to the court.'

Of the Clerk, Lord Justice Tucker wrote, 'He should no doubt have taken a firmer line with his chairman at the outset and advised him to proceed in the County Court or at any rate to wait until the next ordinary court day, but he had been a justice for twenty-six years and having seen him I doubt whether such advice would have had any practical result.'

This raises the interesting question as to how far a Clerk is bound to obey the orders of his justices. For a justice who happens to be the chairman of the bench to order the Clerk to summon a special court to deal with proceedings in which he, the chairman, was to be a party, was surely an order he could not properly give. If the Clerk had refused to obey, it is difficult to imagine that the justices as a body would have taken any action against him. A justice who is a party to a case not only has no right to take part in the adjudication but also has no right to give the Clerk orders as to how the case is to be conducted. Such orders would properly come from the justices constituting the bench, and it is unlikely that they would insist on proceeding with the hearing at a special court if the Clerk pointed out to them the inadvisability of doing so.

The moral of both these cases seems to be this. If a magistrate is asked to sit at a court other than at the place where the magistrates usually sit or at a time other than the time at which they usually sit, he should make certain that there is very good reason for the departure from custom; and if he has the slightest misgiving refuse to take part in the proceedings.

CHAPTER 7

CIVIL OR CRIMINAL?

PROCEEDINGS which come before the courts fall into two great divisions – criminal and civil. The division is vital and fundamental.

Several pages may be wasted in hunting an exact definition of crime to earth, but there is no need to waste them here. For our purpose it is sufficient to say that crimes are acts which are harmful to the welfare of us all as a community and for that reason may be punished by death, imprisonment, or fines. They range from the gravest offences against the commonweal such as treason and murder to infringements of byelaws and regulations for the pettiest matters – as, for example, allowing a dog to be out without a collar or too boisterous merrymaking in a motor-coach.

Civil proceedings comprise all other cases triable in the courts. They are for the most part proceedings brought by one individual against another on the ground that he personally has been wronged. He comes into court to ask that his wrongs may be righted. These actions cover the whole field of human activity – the enforcement of broken contracts, damages and compensation for injuries, petitions for divorce, maintenance orders, custody of children, unpaid debts. Most of these are not triable in the magistrates' courts at all. They can be heard only in the High Court or in the County Courts. Those which can be tried by the magistrates are dealt with in the concluding chapters of this book.

Often, of course, both criminal and civil proceedings arise from the same incidents or acts. The reckless motorist may be charged with the criminal offence of dangerous driving which is harmful to the community in general and sued for damages by the pedestrian whom the motorist's bad driving has harmed in particular. A husband may be charged with neglecting to maintain his family whereby they became chargeable to the county council and at the same time his

wife may institute civil proceedings against him for a maintenance order on the ground of desertion or of neglecting to
maintain her.

In each case both the community and an individual is
aggrieved. The community's remedy is criminal; the individual's civil.

It is of great practical importance always to keep the
distinction between criminal and civil matters clearly before
us. To a chance visitor to the court there may seem to be no
difference in the way they are tried, but in fact there are great
differences.

To begin with, if a magistrate thinks it right to do so he
may issue a warrant to bring a person charged with a crime
before his court, no matter how trivial the offence he is
alleged to have committed. In civil proceedings it is only in
exceptional circumstances that he can grant a warrant of
arrest in the first instance.

But it is during the course of the hearing in court that the
most important differences between civil and criminal proceedings arise.

In criminal proceedings the liberty, the reputation, and in
some cases the life of the defendant may be at stake. The
law therefore insists that its ministers – judges and magistrates alike – shall be much more careful in accepting
evidence and far more cautious in concluding that he is
guilty than had he been brought into court on an analogous
civil proceeding.

If the defendant to a criminal charge pleads 'Not guilty'
every part of the charge must be strictly proved by the
prosecution. In civil proceedings both sides may make
admissions which often save the attendance of witnesses and
narrow the proceedings to those points upon which the
parties do not agree. Compare, for instance, a criminal
charge of bigamy and a wife's civil complaint of desertion.
In the first both the marriages must be strictly proved, though
the defendant may admit that they took place. In the second,
it is usually sufficient for the wife to say that she married the

defendant. She need not prove the marriage unless it is the defendant's case that there was no valid ceremony and for that reason he would not be liable to maintain her.

Then too there are many special rules of evidence affecting criminal procedure from which civil matters are free. Some of these are outlined in Chapters 11 to 16. In particular is it worth noticing that in most criminal prosecutions a wife cannot be called to give evidence against her husband or a husband against his wife, whilst in civil cases this prohibition does not exist.

Most important of all, judges and magistrates must be less easily satisfied of the guilt of a person charged with a criminal offence than of the liability of a person against whom civil proceedings are taken. Again remembering what the person accused of a criminal offence may have at stake, the Law insists that its ministers shall take no risks by acting upon insufficient evidence.

It therefore insists that in criminal proceedings the courts must be satisfied 'beyond reasonable doubt' of the guilt of the accused. If his accusers cannot prove the charge up to the hilt, the evidence must be so strong that no one could reasonably feel that in convicting him there would be the possibility of a miscarriage of justice.

In civil proceedings on the other hand where there is at least no immediate risk of imprisonment the standard of proof required is not so high. In these the magistrates may act upon what they think is reasonably probable. If after hearing both sides they come to the conclusion that one is more likely to be true than the other, then they may exercise their powers accordingly.

The difference lies in the way the law requires a court to look at criminal and civil cases after all the evidence has been heard. In a criminal prosecution the courts listen to the evidence called by the person who makes the charge and his witnesses. They then listen to the defendant if he wishes to make a statement or give evidence and to any witnesses he may call. After hearing all this, they should then ask themselves – not, 'Which of these stories is the more likely to be true?' but 'Has the prosecutor proved his case sufficiently conclusively that I may be reasonably sure that I shall not run the risk of convicting an innocent man?'

In a civil case they hear the evidence of the person who makes the complaint. If they feel that this is strong enough to justify it, they call upon the defendant to make his reply. If he fails to reply then the day goes against him by default. If he does reply, they may ask themselves 'Which of these stories is the more likely to be true?'

In many civil cases, if the courts were to insist upon the same high standard of proof demanded in a criminal prosecution, the complainant would never be able to attain it. In matrimonial cases, for example, the witnesses are often only the wife who complains and the husband who denies her complaints. The magistrates must do their best to find out which is telling the truth and act in favour of the side upon which they think the evidence preponderates.

In cases such as these, it may be said, 'Here is oath against oath. I cannot possibly say which side is telling the truth and which is lying.' Sometimes this is true but it is a refuge in which the courts should not take shelter too readily or too often. 'The court is not relieved from the duty of weighing the evidence,' said Lord Birkenhead in deciding such a case of deadlock between husband and wife as we have described, 'merely because the parties who alone know the truth, tell different stories, one of which at least cannot be true' (*C*. (otherwise *H*.) v. *C*. [1921], P. 399).

His Lordship went on to give judgement in favour of the wife saying 'Her story may be true; his cannot be'. That was a civil proceeding. We must not presume to conjecture what a Lord High Chancellor would or would not say in other circumstances, but we may be sure that he would never have used similar terms in summing up a criminal charge. He would never have said, 'The prosecutor's story may be true; the defendant's cannot be'. The prosecutor's story, no matter what the defendant's may have been, must convince the court that it not only may be true but is true 'beyond reasonable doubt'.

It has sometimes been thought that proceedings instituted in consequence of adultery and connivance at adultery are an exception to the general rule for civil proceedings and that in such cases as these the courts must demand the same high degree of proof as for a criminal offence. *Ginesi* v. *Ginesi* [1948], P. 179.

Some doubt has since been thrown on this view in *Davis* v. *Davis* [1950], P. 125, where Lord Justice Denning suggested that a sufficient test was laid down by the Matrimonial Causes Act, 1950, Section 4, which requires the court to be 'satisfied on the evidence that the case has been proved.'

Finally there is a great difference in the powers given to the courts in dealing with criminal and civil cases.

One object of criminal proceedings is the punishment of the offender either by making him pay a fine, by imprisoning him, or in some cases by taking his life. Another is the reform of the criminal as, for example, by the use of the probation system which is explained in Chapter 24.

The object of civil proceedings is neither punishment nor reform. It is to make the black sheep of the community do what the white sheep do without compulsion. A husband does not maintain his wife. The court will make an order that in future he shall pay her so much per week. An employer wrongfully dismisses a workman without notice. The court will make an order compelling him to pay the servant his wages for the period he was entitled to notice. Mr A. has not paid his income tax. The court will make an order that he pay it and if he does not will sell his furniture or send him to prison for contempt of the order.

Looking at criminal and civil matters from this angle, we see again that the fundamental difference between them is that the first is a means devised to protect the community generally whilst the second is a protection or a means of reparation for the individual in particular.

But you may say, 'These differences are appreciable but

very theoretical. Is there any practical way in which we can recognize the distinction?'

There is a practical way. The two proceedings are given distinctive technical labels which in most Acts of Parliament – certainly all modern Acts – are accurately used.

Thus criminal proceedings are launched by what is called an 'information', a statement setting out shortly the facts which it is claimed disclose an 'offence'. The person who launches it is called a 'prosecutor' or 'informant' and the whole enterprise is termed a 'prosecution'.

Civil proceedings begin with a 'complaint' by a 'complainant' and the proceedings generally are referred to as a 'complaint'. They usually end with an 'order' being made or refused by the court to make some money payment or to do something, such as to put an end to a nuisance, to keep a dangerous dog under proper control, or to pay a weekly sum for the maintenance of a dependant.

If a criminal prosecution is successful the defendant is found guilty and if he is fined or imprisoned he is said to be 'convicted'. These terms are never used in civil complaints.

The Act of Parliament under which the magistrates are asked to adjudicate will usually betray the character of the proceedings because it will almost certainly contain some of these terms.

Thus if we open *Stone* under the Chapter 'Railways' we shall find four sub-headings in succession all using the word 'offences' and we shall frequently notice the term 'on conviction'. Clearly here everything is criminal.

On the other hand, turning to the Chapter headed 'Labour Laws' we shall find that proceedings under the second section of the Chapter headed 'Employers and Workmen Act, 1875', are obviously civil proceedings. The court whilst dealing with disputes under the Act is 'deemed to be a court of civil jurisdiction' and if it finds in favour of one side to a dispute, it may make certain 'orders'.

In a few old Acts we shall find that these distinctive labels have been applied without the discrimination with which they are now used. Thus Section 12 of the Trade Union Act, 1871, which allows proceedings to be taken by a Trade Union against a member or official who has withheld or appropriated its funds, begins by describing the proceedings as a 'complaint' and ends by allowing the court to make 'an order upon the person so convicted' which if not obeyed is punishable 'by imprisonment up to three months'.

In this case the judges have decided that the magistrates have a discretion and may deal with the matter either as a criminal offence or as a civil debt.

Such Acts, however, are rare and are gradually disappearing as old statutes are replaced by new.

CHAPTER 8

THE CLASSIFICATION OF CRIME

OUR forefathers divided crimes into three great classes: treasons, felonies, and misdemeanours.

Treasons are crimes against the Queen and the state; compassing the Queen's death, adhering to her enemies and the like.

Felonies are crimes which from the earliest days of all civilized communities have been instinctively recognized as so dangerous to the authority of the state as to justify it in taking special measures – that is, criminal proceedings – against those who committed them.

We find felonies in all the early collections of laws; in the Ten Commandments, in the Twelve Tables on which the Roman Law was founded, in our own unwritten 'common law' of Anglo-Saxon days. They are those actions so gross and brutal that everyone regards them as crimes without question – murder, manslaughter, burglary, robbery, stealing.

Misdemeanours were a later development. They came in with the sharpening wits of a people steadily becoming more civilized. Often pen and paper were needed to commit them and equally to describe them. They are for the most part less obviously crimes than felonies. They are offences involving little risk of a breach of the peace because many are committed by fraud so that the victim does not know till later that he has been cheated.

Most misdemeanours have been created by Act of Parliament. All crimes which are not treasons or felonies fall into this residuary class. If an Act is passed creating new criminal offences and it does not describe them as felonies or treasons, then we may take it for granted that they are misdemeanours. Parliament only rarely now creates a new felony or treason.

This old classification is still important in the higher

criminal courts of Assize and Quarter Sessions and to the policeman on his beat, but is of much less moment to magistrates and the summary courts.

A police officer, for example, may arrest a person he has good reason to think has committed a felony, but he must in most cases apply to a magistrate for a warrant if the offence is only a misdemeanour.

In the higher criminal courts the procedure is not quite the same for the trial of a felony as for that of a misdemeanour. In the magistrates' courts the procedure is the same for both.

To this old classification must now be added a new one. For the summary courts it is much the more important.

This latter classification divides crime into Indictable Offences and Non-Indictable Offences. It is important to define them carefully.

An indictable offence is a crime which, when the person charged with committing it first appears in Court, cannot be dealt with by magistrates but must be committed by them for trial at Assizes or Quarter Sessions.

A non-indictable or summary offence is a crime which, when the person charged with committing it first appears in Court, can be dealt with only by magistrates summarily.

The importance of the clause, 'when the person charged with committing it first appears in Court', which occurs in both these definitions, will appear later.

Indictable offences consist of all treasons, all felonies, and the most serious misdemeanours.

All other misdemeanours are non-indictable offences.

But there is a more practical and definite means of distinguishing between indictable and non-indictable offences.

If Parliament intends an offence to be treated as non-indictable, the Act creating it will say so. It will use words or phrases which will indicate that it is an offence to be dealt with by the magistrates.

Thus Section 42 of the Offences Against the Person Act, 1861, creates the offence of common assault punishable with a maximum imprisonment of two months. The section also tells us how the offence is to be tried – 'two Justices of the Peace may hear and determine such offence'. Clearly this is an offence which Parliament intends to be dealt with summarily.

Expressions which convey the same intention are 'triable summarily', 'before two or more justices', 'on summary conviction', and so on.

Phrases containing the word 'summary', of course, mean a trial which takes place without delay. In our law it is synonymous with trial before magistrates in the summary courts. The Acts which formerly governed the procedure of the magistrates' courts were entitled 'The Summary Jurisdiction Acts', and have now been replaced by the Magistrates' Courts Act, 1952.

In long modern Acts of Parliament it is now customary to describe certain actions or conduct as 'offences' and towards the end of the Act will be found a 'prosecution section' which tells us how Parliament intends these offences to be tried. We have already seen an example of this in the case of the Road Traffic Act, 1930, in Chapter 2, page 13.

If we can find no Act stating that a particular offence is to be tried summarily, then it follows that it must be an indictable offence which cannot be tried by the magistrates.

Thus, for example, if we turn up the chapter in *Stone* headed 'Person (Offences against the)', we shall find a number of sections of Acts of Parliament quoted which define serious criminal offences: abduction, abortion, bigamy, murder, manslaughter. But we shall find no words in these sections which show that they are to be dealt with by the magistrates in the summary courts and the absence of any such authority means that they cannot be tried in them.

Yet many indictable offences are dealt with by the magistrates. Nearly all petty larcenies, for example. This brings us to the reason why in our definition of an indictable offence we added the words 'when the person charged with committing it first appears in court'.

And the reason is that there are a number of indictable offences which, if the defendants agree in the course of the proceedings, the magistrates are allowed to try instead of sending them on to a judge and jury for trial.

The magistrates are empowered to try adults charged with such offences by the Magistrates' Courts Act, 1952, Section 19. It is worth reading carefully. First of all, it applies only to a selection of indictable offences which is set out in the First Schedule to the Act. A fairly exhaustive list of these offences is given on page 213. Then the section sets out the circumstances which will justify the magistrates in trying a charge which normally should go to a higher court – 'having regard to any representations made in the presence of the accused by the prosecutor or made by the accused, and to the nature of the case, that the punishment that the court has power to inflict under this section would be adequate and that the circumstances do not make the offence one of serious character and do not for other reasons require trial on indictment'.

If, after considering these points, the magistrates decide it would be proper for them to undertake the trial, the accused must be asked if he consents. If he does not consent the charge remains an indictable offence which can be dealt with only by the higher courts. He may be asked to consent at any time during the trial, but the moment he is asked and agrees the charge drops out of the category of indictable offences and is dealt with in all respects as if it were a non-indictable offence.

Where the proceedings have been instituted by the Director of Public Prosecutions or a government or local authority, the consent of the prosecution must also be obtained before the magistrates ask the defendant to consent. The defendant must also be warned that if he is convicted summarily and it then turns out that he has a bad character, the magistrates in pursuance of the Magistrates' Courts Act, 1952, Sect. 29, may commit him for sentence to quarter sessions if they think their powers of punishment are inadequate.

In just the same way as there are indictable offences which if the defendant consents may be tried summarily, so there are a number of non-indictable offences upon which the defendant has the right to claim to be tried by a jury at Assizes or Quarter Sessions. These offences are with one or two exceptions those non-indictable offences for which a maximum of over three months' imprisonment may be imposed by a summary court without the option of a fine.

Thus, for example, a man charged with being drunk has no choice. He must submit to the jurisdiction of the magistrates before whom he is charged. But if instead he were charged with driving a motor-car whilst under the influence of drink he would be liable to four months' imprisonment if dealt with by the magistrates. As he runs the risk of so heavy a sentence he has been given the right to choose between the bench of magistrates and a judge and jury.

Both these charges when they first come into court are non-indictable. It is only when the defendant makes his claim in the more serious charge that he raises it from the non-indictable class to the higher indictable class.

This procedure is regulated by the Magistrates' Courts Act, 1952, Section 25. This also is worth reading carefully. Notice that a person charged with an assault is not given the right. In another instance the right has been expressly taken away by Parliament where a man is charged with knowingly living on the earnings of prostitution or of persistently soliciting for immoral purposes in a public place contrary to the Vagrancy Act, 1898, s. 1.

It is the duty of the court to tell the defendant of this right and then to ask him 'Do you desire to be tried by a jury?' If he replies 'No' or makes no reply, the charge remains non-indictable and the court proceeds to try it (*R. v. Kakelo* [1923], 2 K.B. 797).

A list of offences in which this claim may be made appears on page 218.

Finally we must notice a third class of offences which may be both indictable and non-indictable. One example is the charge of assault. On page 47 we have quoted the Act which made common assault triable summarily, but the charge is also an indictable offence and in proper circumstances it may be dealt with as such.

But for the most part these offences are a recent phase of legislative draughtsmanship. We shall find a number in the Road Traffic Act, 1930. Thus Section 11 (1) makes dangerous driving an offence punishable '(a) On summary conviction [by] a fine not exceeding £50 or [by] imprisonment for a term not exceeding four months; (b) on conviction on indictment [by] imprisonment for a term not exceeding two years'.

In such cases who decides whether the charge shall be dealt with summarily or upon indictment?

We shall find the answer to this question in the Magistrates' Courts Act, 1952, s. 18.

If, at the opening of the proceedings, the prosecutor asks for the charge to be tried summarily, the court may determine to do so. If, however, the magistrates think it is an offence which should be tried at Assizes or Quarter Sessions, the prosecution must bow to their ruling. If the prosecution is silent at the outset, then the charge must be treated as an indictable offence, but after the proceedings have begun, if the magistrates consider it a charge they can try summarily, they may do so after hearing anything that the parties may have to say on this point. Where, however, the prosecution is carried on by the Director of Public Prosecutions the magistrates must not deal with the case without his consent.

The defendant himself will, of course, have a voice in the matter if he has a right to claim trial by jury by virtue of Section 25 of the same Act. In such cases he will have the last word. If he elects to be tried by a jury, both prosecutor and magistrates must accede to his claim.

It is not often that such charges are committed for trial. The real reason for the creation of this double-track class with a procedure as engagingly simple as the permanent way at Willesden Junction is so that these lesser offences can be joined to indictments for wounding and the like. If the major charges fail, the jury may convict on the lesser. Otherwise the acquittal on the greater charges may mean either the escape of the defendant altogether or the commencement of new proceedings before magistrates upon the minor charges.

The contents of the last two chapters may be summarized in the accompanying diagram:

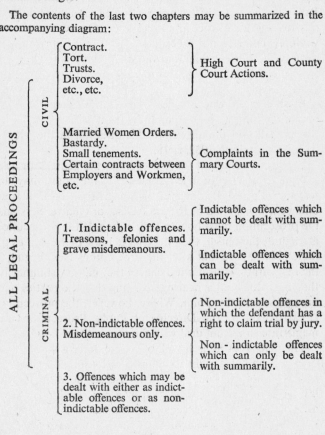

ALL LEGAL PROCEEDINGS

CIVIL
- Contract.
  Tort.
  Trusts.
  Divorce,
  etc., etc.
  } High Court and County Court Actions.

- Married Women Orders.
  Bastardy.
  Small tenements.
  Certain contracts between Employers and Workmen, etc.
  } Complaints in the Summary Courts.

CRIMINAL
1. Indictable offences. Treasons, felonies and grave misdemeanours.
  { Indictable offences which cannot be dealt with summarily.
  Indictable offences which can be dealt with summarily.

2. Non-indictable offences. Misdemeanours only.
  { Non-indictable offences in which the defendant has a right to claim trial by jury.
  Non-indictable offences which can only be dealt with summarily.

3. Offences which may be dealt with either as indictable offences or as non-indictable offences.

CHAPTER 9

SUMMARY TRIAL OF OFFENCES

CRIMINAL proceedings may begin in three ways.

The offender may be arrested by the police, in which case the first that the magistrates will know of him will be when he appears before the court.

Or he may be brought before the court by a summons or upon a warrant.

In both these cases, an application must be made to a magistrate. For this purpose, one magistrate is sufficient. The person who makes the application is called an informant. His statement to the magistrate setting out the details of the offence he alleges has been committed is called an information.

The application is usually made on a day when the court is sitting. But it need not be made in court. It is often convenient to take it in the office of the clerk of the court or in the magistrate's home.

If the informant is asking for a summons the information in most cases need only be verbal, but if he is asking for a warrant he must put the allegations he is making into writing. He must sign the statement and then swear or affirm before the magistrate he is asking to grant the warrant that the information is true to his own knowledge or to the best of his belief.

The Law insists upon magistrates taking these safeguards before issuing a warrant because whereas a summons merely directs a person to appear at court upon a particular day at a stated hour the warrant is directed to a constable and it tells him to arrest the person accused and bring him into court as soon as possible. In permitting magistrates to interfere with the liberty of a subject, the law insists that they shall do so only after taking all precautions against vexatious and possibly groundless accusations.

Whether a summons or a warrant shall be issued is a

matter for the magistrate's discretion, though it is usual for the informant to suggest which of the two he thinks most suitable. A good rule is 'Never grant a warrant if a summons is likely to be equally effective'. Where the offence alleged is a small one, or even where the offence is grave, if the address of the accused person is known and it is unlikely that he will make an attempt to run away, a summons should be issued. Where the offence is grave or where the defendant has no known place of abode or may disappear if it comes to his knowledge that criminal proceedings are in contemplation, it is usual to grant a warrant.

The magistrates are of course entitled to refuse to grant even a summons. But they must do so on what is termed 'judicial' grounds – as, for example, if they think that what is alleged in the information does not amount to the offence which the informer says has been committed. It would be quite wrong to refuse it because they thought Parliament ought not to have created such an offence or because they think in the particular circumstances foreshadowed in the information no proceedings ought to be taken.

On the other hand, if the magistrates consider that the information laid is simply vexatious and that it would be in the public interest to refuse it, they are entitled to do so. It is only rarely that an application can be refused on these grounds. A magistrate was upheld in his refusal many years ago when an improper attempt was made to obtain a summons against a Jewish baker for selling bread on a Sunday. The baker served a large Jewish community and closed his shop on Saturdays, the Jewish Sabbath. The magistrate appears to have scented that the proceedings were taken not to vindicate the law but out of petty spite. His refusal to lend his powers to such an enterprise was upheld by the judges (*R.* v. *Bros* (1901), 66 J.P. 54).

When a warrant is granted the information is a separate document and is preserved by the clerk of the court, whilst the warrant is handed to the police for execution. The information for a summons may also be on a separate sheet but is often combined with the summons thus:

'Information has this day been laid before me that you on 1st May, 19—, at High Street, Blackton, did keep a dog without having in force a licence authorizing you to do so.

'Contrary to Dog Licences Act, 1867, s. 8.

'You are therefore summoned to appear, etc.'

The information for a warrant is usually set out in greater detail, but in granting either a warrant or a summons the magistrates must be careful to notice three things – the offence itself, when it took place, and where it took place.

The offence alleged should be set out in the words of the Act of Parliament under which the proceedings are taken. The Act and the section or sections creating the offence should be correctly cited. The information should show that on the face of it an offence has been committed, but it is not necessary for the informant to go further than this and show that the defendant is unable to avail himself of any special defence permitted by the law.

It is important to see too that each information is for one offence only, though the summons may contain two or more offences. For indictable offences this rule does not apply; an information may contain several alleged offences and so may a summons or warrant issued upon it.

The information must clearly state when the alleged offence took place. This is important because as a general rule proceedings cannot be taken against a person for a summary offence more than six months after it was committed. Thus if someone asks on 1 August for a summons against a person for obstructing the High Street on the 1 January the answer will be 'You are out of time.'

In some cases the informant will be able to retort 'But the six months limit does not apply in my case. Parliament has allowed me longer.' This is so, for example, under the National Health and Unemployment Insurance Acts. Where a special limitation is claimed, the magistrates should ask to see the Act and section relied upon.

Some offences are termed 'continuing offences'. The best example of them is the 'Nuisance' which may have begun years ago but still continues. Proceedings against offences of this kind may be taken for any day within six months of their existence.

Thirdly the place where it is alleged the offence occurred must be clearly described, because upon this depends the jurisdiction of the court granting the summons. Though the Magistrates' Courts Act, 1952, s. 1 (2) allows a magistrate to issue a warrant upon certain rare occasions when a person suspected of having committed an offence outside his area happens to be within it, he is not entitled to grant a summons for a summary offence which has not been committed within the jurisdiction of his court. This extends to the boundaries of the borough or county for which he is a justice and, in order not to embroil rival courts in arguments about a yard, to five hundred yards beyond those boundaries.

If a river or harbour divides one district from another, any offence committed on them may be dealt with in either court.

If an offence is committed upon a journey 'in or upon any carriage, cart or vehicle or on board any vessel', the offender may be tried in any jurisdiction through which the journey was made. Thus, if upon a train running from Paddington to Penzance a passenger wrongfully pulls the communication cord at Reading he may find himself brought before the magistrates at Plymouth, or indeed before any of the many benches through whose territory the train passed.

The warrant as we have seen is handed to the police to be executed. It too, of course, must contain the charge made against the person to be arrested so that he will know what is alleged against him. It may be 'backed for bail'. This means that besides directing a police officer to arrest a person it will also direct his release pending court proceedings on bail either in his own recognizances or upon finding sureties. These directions are sometimes printed at the foot of the warrant or on the back of it, and hence we speak of such a warrant as 'backed for bail'.

Unless the informant – usually a police officer – has some good reason for opposing this backing – as, for example, that the accused will abscond or will interfere with the witnesses for the prosecution – a warrant should always be backed so that as little injury as possible will be done to the accused whilst he is still unconvicted. If later he is acquitted it will not be felt that an innocent person has been kept unnecessarily under lock and key.

The summons is a more gentlemanly weapon. It is a notification to a person that it is alleged that he has committed an offence against an Act of Parliament at a given time and at a given place. It then goes on to summon him to appear at a magistrates' court at a stated time on a stated day. It must be signed or stamped at the foot by the magistrate who grants it.

The next step is to see that the summons is put into the accused person's hands, or, if this cannot be done, is left where it is reasonably certain it will reach him – that is, by leaving it with some person at his 'last or most usual place of abode'.

This is called 'serving' a summons. The 'service' is important because most non-indictable offences can be dealt with in the absence of the defendant if it is proved that the 'service' is 'good' – that is to say, it has been made in accordance with the Magistrates' Courts Act, 1952. If the service is not in accordance with them, the proceedings cannot be begun and the magistrates may then in their discretion issue a warrant of arrest. The abortive summons is entered in the register as 'Not served'.

Some Acts of Parliament allow a summons to be served by sending it by registered post or by pinning it to the door of the house where the defendant lives, but this applies only to the offences under these particular Acts. If no special directions are given as to how summonses are to be served under an Act, the summons must be served in accordance with the Magistrates' Courts Act, 1952 as described above.

Rule 76 of the Magistrates' Courts Rules now allows all

summonses to be served by sending them by registered post, but the magistrates can regard this service as 'good' only if the defendant makes some response which shows that he has received the summons – either by turning up at the hearing, or by the appearance of an advocate on his behalf, or by acknowledging the receipt of the summons in writing; the latter, of course, most commonly taking the form of a letter of explanation.

The practice of writing a letter in answer to a summons instead of the defendant appearing himself is a growing one. The days have passed when almost all persons summoned to appear before a bench of magistrates lived near the court. This is particularly true of motorists summoned for minor breaches of the Road Traffic Acts. If they were compelled to attend, the cost in fares and loss of time would often far exceed the amount of the fine imposed.

In some cases, of course, it is most desirable that the defendant should appear; where, for example, he has the right to elect to be tried by a jury; in all cases where he may be sent to prison without the option of a fine; or when the magistrates consider it proper that he should be present for special reasons arising in a particular case. Even appearance by an advocate may not be sufficient in these circumstances.

Should the defendant fail to appear in such a case, the magistrates usually adjourn the proceedings, sending him notice of the date of the adjournment with an intimation that his presence is essential. Should he fail to appear then, the magistrates may very properly issue a warrant to compel his attendance.

CHAPTER 10

IN COURT

We all have to be judges of something – of our own conduct and interests, of the work and conduct of others. Judges and magistrates stand out from the commonalty because they have been chosen by the State to try their fellow citizens and administer the Law.

All honest judges go about their judging in its essentials in the same way. They hear the story of the citizen who is aggrieved and his witnesses and then the answer of the defendant and his witnesses. Having maintained an air of complete impartiality if not of impassivity throughout the recital, they then give their decision.

Many people think that to act in this way is all that the State should require of its judges – no books, no clever lawyers, no past decisions to trammel present problems, no long delays, no ruinous expense, no pettifogging technicalities; the cadi beneath the date palm, the Anglo-Saxon king beneath the Anglo-Saxon oak; such has been the summer's day dream of law reformers down the ages. Only with an effort do we bring ourselves to realize that there is another side to this picture.

For if the State left its judges and magistrates such a free hand as this they would be able to decide what actions should be regarded as offences and what should not be, how offences should be tried apart from the elementary rule that both sides must be heard, what the witnesses should be allowed to say and what not, who should be called as witnesses and who should not, and finally what should be done about it all in the way of punishment or amendment.

One of two benches for example both equally well-meaning and honest might make it illegal to be absent from church and punish heavily anyone who did not attend. The other sitting in the next town might make it illegal to attend church and visit penalties on those who did.

And always we are up against the problem that if we start with fair-minded and honest judges and magistrates we cannot be sure that they will in spite of all temptations and with advancing age remain so. As the years go by most people mellow with ripening experience and so become more suited than before to occupy the judgement seat. But some grow into crabbed misanthropes totally out of sympathy with the succeeding generations they have to try. Solomon old may disappoint the promise of Solomon young.

The State has therefore been compelled to fetter the discretion of its judges. The law keeps a hold upon them no less firm than upon those on whom they are empowered to sit in judgement. We have already seen the first of the means by which this is done. Magistrates cannot punish any person unless he has committed an act which the law allows them to punish or to compel him to do something unless a statute allows them to compel him to do so. A bench may disapprove of dancing. They cannot punish any of their fellow citizens for dancing. They may disapprove of empty pews at church. They cannot compel anyone to attend service. The law is silent on these matters and for that reason they are powerless.

We have seen too how the judges take a hand in this control. When once they have held that a word, a phrase, a section of an Act is to be interpreted in a particular way the magistrates are bound by this ruling until it is changed by some higher authority.

Again, the very fact that lay magistrates sit in pairs if not in greater numbers is another fetter upon their discretion. Plurality upon the bench tends towards balance, compromise, and the elimination of extreme views and measures.

But the law goes further than this. It places a number of other restrictions upon the courts when dealing with criminal charges which we shall consider in the next chapters.

Firstly, it will allow them to try a person only in a certain way. It regulates the manner in which a court is to be run and how a case shall be tried. This is what lawyers call 'the Law of Procedure'.

Secondly, it will allow only certain persons to be called as witnesses. This is part of the 'Law of Evidence'.

Thirdly, it will not allow those who can be called as witnesses always to tell the court everything they know about the charge which has brought them there. This is another part of the 'Law of Evidence'.

Finally, it will not allow the courts to convict the accused unless the evidence has satisfied them beyond reasonable doubt that he is guilty.

You may feel by this time that the courts are not only fettered but bound hand and foot. In practice we shall find it is not so – or shall we say, the bonds make themselves felt only upon occasion. Often magistrates will go through a whole sitting without once being made aware of the restraints we have just noticed. But they are there, always with us, just as the force of gravity is always with us, keeping anchored to the good earth the judgement seat, the magisterial person, and the court register. If the newly-fledged magistrate lets himself go too boldly, be sure that sooner or later these forces of judicial gravity will bring him down to ground again.

CHAPTER 11

PROCEDURE

WE can give the outline of a criminal trial before magistrates in a few words.

If the defendant pleads 'not guilty', the informant calls his witnesses and the defendant is invited to question them after they have given their evidence. If when all the witnesses for the prosecution have been heard, the magistrates think the informant has proved the alleged offence if the case should stop at this point, they must then invite the defendant to give his answer. He can do this by making an unsworn statement from the place he has been occupying in court during the trial. After this, or instead of this, he can go into the witness box and give evidence as the witnesses for the prosecution have done. Then he too may call witnesses. The magistrates must then decide whether to convict or acquit.

To this brief outline we must add some comments.

First of all, it must be remembered that however trivial the charge the defendant is actually on trial for a criminal offence. He is, to use the phrase of the old criminal lawyers, 'in peril' of a fine and perhaps imprisonment and therefore all the proceedings must take place in 'open court' – that is to say, as many of the public as wish to attend and as the court room can conveniently hold must be allowed in so that they can see for themselves that their fellow citizen is being tried fairly and according to law. The fellow citizen may wish them anywhere but present to witness his predicament, but that makes no difference. The only occasions when the law allows the public to be shut out from a criminal trial are when a witness under seventeen is giving evidence upon a charge against decency or morality; in the Juvenile and Domestic Courts; and in proceedings where state secrets would be revealed if the public were admitted. In the first three cases, press reporters are permitted to remain so that the safeguard of the open court is still largely maintained.

At the beginning of the trial the defendant is asked whether he pleads guilty or not guilty. The charge should be read to the defendant and he is then asked to plead. This is usually done by the clerk. It is most important to see that the defendant understands the charge and that if he pleads guilty he does so without reservation. If there is the slightest doubt whether he understands exactly what charge is being made against him or if he tries to equivocate, a plea of not guilty should be enregistered.

If the defendant pleads guilty no witnesses need be called and the magistrates pass straight on to the question of how they shall deal with him.

Sometimes after a defendant has pleaded guilty, it will be found from statements he makes that in fact he has misunderstood the charge and should not have pleaded guilty at all. This frequently happens where a defendant is charged with some offence involving not only physical action but mental intent such as stealing or malicious damage. He thinks he is guilty because he has committed the act but upon investigation it often turns out that he vigorously contests that he did the act intentionally. It is the intent which transforms the act into a criminal offence, and the moment that this element of the offence is questioned, the court should replace the plea of guilty with one of not guilty and begin afresh.

Of course, a defendant who pleads guilty unequivocally after having the charge against him made clear, cannot afterwards ask to plead not guilty. In *R.* v. *Campbell* ex parte Hoy (1953) 117 J.P. 36 a woman was charged with knowingly harbouring uncustomed goods, to wit, 262 pairs of American nylon stockings with intent to defraud Her Majesty of the duties thereon. She was sentenced to four months imprisonment. Later a solicitor applied on behalf of the woman to be allowed to change the plea to 'not guilty'. The magistrate agreed to this, but upon appeal the judges held that 'the magistrate having heard and determined the case and convicted was functus officio and had no power to allow the plea to be changed'.

This case may be contrasted with *R.* v. *Durham Quarter Sessions*, ex parte Virgo (1952) 116 J.P. 157 where a man pleaded guilty to stealing a cycle. When asked if he had anything to say he replied, 'I thought it was my mate's cycle. My mate said, "Take it home!" My mate's bike is identical.' On appeal it was held that here the magistrates should have entered a plea of not guilty in place of the plea of guilty.

Contrasting the two cases, Lord Goddard said, 'If there had been any ambiguity in her plea, Miss Campbell would have entered a plea of not guilty, but this was a perfectly unambiguous, unequivocal plea of guilty, not like the pleas that are so often made, and as was the plea in the *R.* v. *Durham Quarter Sessions* case, where a man was charged with receiving stolen property and in effect said, "Guilty of receiving but I did not know they were stolen," which amounted to a plea of not guilty.'

Nowadays increasingly few of the many defendants summoned turn up. All non-indictable offences can be dealt with in the absence of the defendant, even those under Section 25 of the Magistrates' Courts Act, 1952, to which we referred in Chapter 8, where the defendant has the right to elect to be tried by a jury. But in all these cases and all other serious non-indictable offences it is highly desirable that the defendant should be present. If in one of these cases he does not appear in answer to a summons, the magistrates may very properly insist upon his attendance, either by adjourning the summons to a later date or by issuing a warrant to compel his appearance.

Where, however, the offence is trivial and the defendant admits that he committed it, there is no reason why the case should not be heard in his absence. The witnesses for the prosecution are sworn and give their evidence. The verdict goes in favour of the informant by default. Sometimes the defendant tries to set up a plea of not guilty by letter. This, of course, cannot be received as evidence by the court and cannot overturn the sworn evidence of witnesses present at court. If there appears to be any substance in what the defendant writes, the best practice in such cases is to adjourn the summons to give the defendant a further opportunity to appear and set up his defence in person.

Both parties are entitled to the services of a solicitor or counsel. Very often in minor charges an advocate appears for a defendant who is unable to come himself. Indeed he may appear in the absence of the defendant even if the defendant is charged with an offence for which he may be sent to prison, and it has been held that a warrant ought not to be issued when a defendant appears by advocate (*Bessel* v. *Wilson* (1853), 17 J.P. 567).

Section 99 of the Magistrates' Courts Act, 1952 provides that 'A party to any proceedings before a magistrates' court may be represented by counsel or solicitor; and an absent party so represented shall be deemed not to be absent'.

This means that in all summary proceedings the court cannot insist upon the personal attendance of the defendant. If he is represented they would not be able to issue a warrant for his arrest to compel his appearance.

A motorist, for example, is summoned for exceeding the speed limit but instructs a solicitor and does not appear himself. Upon conviction the police say they have a record of a number of convictions for similar offences against a person of the same name and the question of disqualification arises. But they are not sure if the defendant is the same man. If he could be compelled to attend a constable might be able to identify him. The court, however, is prohibited by this section from issuing a warrant in such circumstances and the police are left to get over the hurdle in some other way if they can.

But the Section does not apply to proceedings where the Act expressly requires the defendant to be present. He must attend whenever he is charged with an indictable offence though it may be dealt with summarily or with a summary offence if he has the right to claim trial by jury and wishes to exercise his right. He must also appear when charged with failing to pay an affiliation order or any order enforced as an affiliation order. If he has been released on bail after arrest or after an appearance at the Court he must also attend himself.

The magistrates may adjourn a charge until any future date they think fit. They must not of course adjourn it indefinitely to avoid the necessity of coming to a decision at all. If the defendant is in custody they should see that the adjournment is reasonably short. In no case must it exceed eight clear days before conviction. After conviction, however if the offence is an indictable offence being dealt with summarily, the magistrates may remand him in custody for as long as three weeks in pursuance of Section 14 (3) of the Magistrates' Courts Act, 1952 'for the purpose of enabling enquiries to be made or of determining the most suitable method of dealing with the case'. Section 26 of the Act allows a remand for the same length of time of a person convicted of an offence punishable on summary conviction with imprisonment if the magistrates are of opinion that 'an inquiry ought to be made into the accused's physical or mental condition before the method of dealing with him is determined'.

Where either side asks for an adjournment during the hearing of a charge, the magistrates should always grant it unless they think the application is an unreasonable one. A defendant who has been arrested by the police or upon a warrant and therefore has had no opportunity of consulting his friends or advisers or of considering what defences he can set up to the charge made against him should always be granted an adjournment if he asks for it. If it were refused and he were later convicted there and then, it is probable that the conviction would be quashed on appeal. Where the parties have had time to consider their position – as, for example, where there has already been an adjournment or where the defendant appears upon a summons which has given him some days' notice of the charge to be made against him – an adjournment may not be so readily granted. The magistrates ought to enquire into the reasons for the application, because postponement will mean the loss of court time and vexatious delay and expense to the other side who are ready and no doubt anxious to go on. But no one can foresee everything and no one can guard against every eventuality. Where a good reason is given for the application to adjourn, it should be acceded to.

After making some strong criticisms of the action of a County Court judge in refusing a request for an adjournment, a High Court Judge some years ago threw out this valuable rule of practice – 'A litigant who through no fault of his own is prevented from calling his material witness is entitled, subject of course to terms as to costs, to an adjournment as a matter of justice.'

When the defendant has been arrested by the police or upon a warrant the question of bail pending a remand arises. A prisoner is allowed 'bail' when he is released whilst proceedings are being taken against him in the courts. Bail takes the form of a bond technically called a 'recognizance', a word which probably came over with the Conqueror, meaning an acknowledgement. The prisoner 'recognizes' that he and his sureties, if any, owe 'their Sovereign Lady the Queen' (say) £20; but if he appears at 10 a.m. next Thursday at the A — magistrates' court the recognizance shall be void. If he does not turn up he and his sureties can be called upon to pay the sums fixed in their recognizance, whilst in addition, of course, proceedings continue against the prisoner for those charges for which he was originally arrested.

Some of the keenest duels take place between police and prisoner or more often his advocate upon the question of bail.

There is not much guidance to magistrates as to how they should exercise this most important power. The Declaration of Rights forbids 'excessive' bail. A Bail Act, 1898, allows magistrates to grant bail without sureties in their discretion when dealing with indictable offences. Except for this there is little guidance, statutory or judicial.

In his 'Outlines of Criminal Law', Professor Kenny says: 'In exercising their discretion about admitting to bail, the magistrates have simply to consider what likelihood there is of the defendant's failing to appear for trial. That likelihood will be affected by (1) the gravity of the charge; (2) the cogency of the evidence; (3) the wealth of the offender (which renders him both more willing to bear the forfeiture of bail and less willing to bear the disgrace of a conviction); (4) whether the proposed sureties are independent or are likely to have been indemnified by the accused; and (5) the probability of the accused tampering with the Crown's witnesses, if he be at large.'

Bail is granted at some courts much more readily than at others. There is no need to stress of what value the restoration of his liberty may be to an accused person and the advantage it will afford him in the preparation of his defence. He can see his legal advisers as often as necessary instead of having to be content with at best a consultation within prison walls and at worst a hasty conference outside the court room on the eve of trial. He can talk matters over with friends and collect witnesses. The more meagre the means at his disposal, the more vital the need for freedom. The bench must therefore be vigilant to see that the claims of the unrepresented prisoner are as present to their minds as of those of him who can afford a practised advocate to urge them.

Naturally the police often oppose the grant of bail. They may have had some difficulty in finding the prisoner and they may doubt whether if released he will appear again. If the release of a prisoner helps him in his defence it necessarily makes the task of the prosecution more difficult.

Sometimes the police are in this quandary. They object to bail because the defendant has a record of convictions. If he is convicted he knows he will probably have to serve a long sentence. If he is bailed he will be greatly tempted to disappear. Or there may be other charges pending at other courts so that even if he is released upon one charge he may be immediately re-arrested for another.

But if the police disclose these objections to the magistrates, the prisoner may very fairly complain that he is prejudiced because, if the same bench has to try him or to decide if he is to be committed to Assizes or Quarter Sessions, they will now know his past history.

To some extent therefore the magistrates must trust the detective officer who is in charge of the case. If he objects, they should assume that he has good reason for doing so. But if they find he is always objecting to the grant of bail, in all his cases, a post-mortem may justifiably be held at the end of the proceedings when the court has decided whether or not to convict or commit the prisoner. If then it appears that the objection to bail was insubstantial, an intimation may be made to the officer that the court will expect him to be more reasonable in future.

As statistics show, in practice the great majority of bailed prisoners honour their recognizances. Professor Kenny says that in 1927, of three thousand persons bailed only twenty-nine absconded. The insistence upon sureties is usually a sovereign safeguard. The sureties are as a rule intimate friends whom the prisoner would be most reluctant to fail. In certain cases special terms may be imposed, such as to compel the defendant to report daily to the police or to surrender his passport before he is released.

A remand may be granted for many reasons – lack of time, the request of a party for an adjournment, enquiries by the court into the health and antecedents of the defendant – but it must not be ordered as a punishment. Until recently a too popular method of dealing with a convicted prisoner was to remand him for a week in custody 'to let him have a taste of prison' and then release him upon probation.

This is really a device for giving a man seven days' imprisonment whilst depriving him of his right to appeal against the sentence. Not only is this illegal. Not only is it unjust. Far worse than this, it is unsportsmanlike. It is as bad as shooting a sitting bird. Indeed nothing could be more like shooting a sitting bird.

The practice came in for severe criticism in *R.* v. *Brentford Justices; ex parte Muirhead* (1941), 106, J.P. 4. In this case the defendant appeared before a bench of magistrates and the chairman 'without consulting his fellow justices or the clerk' at once remanded him in custody for three weeks. The charge was not put to him, he was not asked to plead, and no evidence was taken. An application for bail was greeted with the remark 'I'll treat them all alike,' inferring that such procedure was commonplace at this court. The maximum penalty for the offence of which the defendant was charged was five pounds.

These extraordinarily high-handed proceedings were unanimously condemned by the judges. Said Lord Caldecote, quoting Lord Hewart, his predecessor in the office of Lord Chief Justice, 'It could not be right for justices to remand an offender in custody for the real, though unavowed, purpose of detaining in prison an offender charged with an offence for which a punishment by imprisonment could not be lawfully ordered'.

Upon the prosecution falls the task of proving the accusation. It is not for the defendant to prove his innocence. The prosecutor must prove the defendant's guilt.

This is called the 'burden or onus of proof'. The prosecutor is called upon to produce witnesses who will give the court evidence of facts which if uncontradicted establish that the defendant has committed the criminal offence of which he is accused.

A moment never comes in a criminal charge as it may come in a civil complaint when the court may say, 'The prosecutor has said the defendant has done this. Now the defendant must show that he has not'. When all the witnesses for the prosecution have been called, the magistrates must ask themselves: 'If the case stopped here, should we consider the prosecutor has proved the charge?' If the answer is

'No' then the defendant should at once be discharged. If the answer is 'Yes' the magistrates should then invite the defendant to tell his story.

In a recent judgement Lord Sankey said, 'Throughout the web of the English Criminal Law one golden thread is always to be seen, that it is the duty of the prosecution to prove the prisoner's guilt subject to the defence of insanity and subject also to any statutory exception. If, at the end of and on the whole of the case, there is a reasonable doubt, created by the evidence given by either the prosecution or the prisoner . . . the prosecution has not made out the case and the prisoner is entitled to an acquittal. No matter what the charge or where the trial, the principle that the prosecution must prove the guilt of the prisoner is part of the common law of England and no attempt to whittle it down can be entertained' (*Woolmington* v. *Director of Public Prosecutions* [1935], A.C. 462).

'Subject to the defence of insanity and subject also to any statutory exception'. The defence of insanity is dealt with in Chapter 33. Statutory exceptions have been made in those charges where the production of evidence of certain facts is an easy matter for the defendant, but is so difficult for the prosecution that if required to produce them proceedings would often have to be abandoned altogether or the evidence would have to be obtained at inordinate cost.

A good example is the Aliens Restriction Act, 1914. If an alien is charged with an offence under the Act, the prosecution is relieved of the burden of proving he is an alien. He is assumed at the outset to be an alien but may successfully defend the charge by proving that he is not.

Again, in a prosecution under the Vagrancy Act, 1898, if the prosecution proves that the defendant has been living with or has been habitually in the company of a prostitute, he will be deemed to be knowingly living on her earnings unless he can satisfy the court to the contrary. But for this provision the burden of proving the defendant's guilty knowledge would be upon the prosecution.

Another exception is the proof of facts peculiarly within the knowledge of the defendant. A motorist, for example, is accused of driving without a policy of insurance. The prosecution prove that he was seen driving a motor vehicle and that he failed upon request to produce a certificate. Whether he is insured or not is a piece of information peculiarly within the knowledge of the motorist. The prosecution if it had to prove he was not insured would have to call representatives from every insurance company. In such circumstances the law holds that the prosecutor has gone sufficiently far in proving the failure to produce and throws upon the defendant the burden of showing that in fact he was covered by a policy (*Williams* v. *Russell* (1933), 97 J.P. 128).

Let us now assume that the trial has reached the point when the prosecution has called its witnesses. As we have already seen, the magistrates must at this point ask themselves, 'Suppose the case ended here, has the evidence proved the charge beyond reasonable doubt?'

If they think it has failed to do so, that is an end of the proceedings. The defendant must be at once acquitted.

But if they think the evidence of the prosecution, standing uncontradicted, established the charge, they must then invite the defendant to tell his story. The word 'invite' is important. The prosecutor must call his witnesses if he wishes to prove the charge. The defendant can please himself whether he will answer the accusation. He cannot be compelled to do so.

He should be told what he can do. He can make an unsworn statement. He can go into the witness box as the witnesses for the prosecution have done and become himself a witness who can be cross-examined by the prosecutor and who can be charged with perjury if he gives false evidence. He can call witnesses on his own behalf.

But the great thing to remember is that the defendant to a criminal charge is not bound to say anything, and his silence if it is deliberate and not mere stage fright or an inability to appreciate the evidence brought against him must be respected. Occasionally a magistrate will be heard putting a string of questions from the bench to the defendant. He has no more right to do this than has the police officer in charge of the case for the prosecution. The most that a magistrate should permit himself to do where the defendant is unrepresented is to suggest that he might like to address the bench upon certain points raised by his accusers.

Of course in deciding whether the defendant is guilty or not guilty the magistrates are entitled and indeed ought to take into account the silence of the defendant or his refusal to be sworn as a witness and to face cross-examination. In minor charges the unsworn testimony of the defendant may be regarded as being almost as worthy of belief as sworn evidence from the witness box. But in more important cases this failure to meet the challenge of the prosecution must tell seriously against the defendant who remains silent or contents himself with a mere statement from the dock which cannot be tested by cross-examination.

So much for the trial of defendants who are individuals.

A phenomenon of to-day's summons lists is the large number of limited companies appearing as defendants. The law regards the corporation – of which the limited company is an example – as a separate entity, something quite apart from its directors, its secretaries, and its shareholders, so that if all these ladies and gentlemen trooped into court in answer to a summons, they would not be regarded as the company, for it is an abstract legal conception wholly distinct from the individuals who are associated with it.

For this reason a special procedure has had to be devised.

Service of summonses for example is effected by leaving them at the registered office of the company or by sending them to that address by registered post.

If the company wishes to put in an appearance it can do so only by solicitor or barrister. The managing director or secretary who so often attends must be told that he is not the defendant and can take no part in the proceedings. Here again is a strict rule often sensibly modified in practice where the company is not contesting the charge. At most courts a representative is allowed to say a few words in mitigation after it has been formally proved.

Where a corporation is charged with a summary offence for which an individual may claim to be tried by a jury the advocate may make the election or a representative especially appointed for the purpose by the corporation may do so. If no advocate or representative appears the charge is dealt with summarily.

Finally the intangibility of the limited company saves it from the rude grasp of the turnkey. If found guilty of an offence, it cannot be sent to prison; but a fine may be imposed and collected if necessary by distraint upon the company's property.

CHAPTER 12

WITNESSES

WE now come to the second restriction upon the discretion or initiative of judges and magistrates in dealing with criminal cases. The law will not allow them to hear the evidence of certain persons at all.

Some people who might normally be expected to give the most valuable evidence are in the lawyers' term 'incompetent'. As compared with those who are 'competent' they are a tiny minority, but, like most minorities, their importance is not to be measured by their numbers.

The group is led by a no less distinguished personage than the Queen herself. She is the Fountain of Justice. When magistrates and judges sit in judgement it is in the Queen's seat that they sit as her deputies. No one can be judge and partisan. So the Queen cannot be called as a witness. She is 'incompetent'.

But anyone else can be called no matter how exalted his station. It will be remembered for example that King Edward VII when Prince of Wales was a witness in the famous baccarat case.

Lunatics and very young children are also incompetent because we cannot rely upon their word.

But a lunatic may be insane upon one matter and perfectly sane on another. If the court is enquiring into a matter upon which he is sane, his evidence may be accepted. Thus a lunatic who thinks he is the head of the Bank of England may be rejected as a witness on financial questions but may be perfectly reliable when giving an account of reckless driving in Threadneedle Street.

In an amusing case where these questions were discussed, one judge observed: 'If the prisoner's counsel could maintain the proposition which he has laid down, that any human being who labours under a delusion of the mind is incompetent as a witness, there would be most widespreading incompetency. Martin Luther, it is said, believed that he had a personal conflict with the Devil. The celebrated Dr Samuel Johnson was convinced that he had heard his mother calling him in a supernatural manner' (*R.* v. *Hill* (1851), 20 L.J.M.C. 222).

To which another judge rejoined: 'The rule contended for would have excluded the evidence of Socrates, for he believed that he had a spirit always prompting him'.

Very young children are obviously unreliable as witnesses. They are as clay in the hands of a skilful cross-examiner and can be coaxed or cajoled into saying anything. Usually children up to the age of seven are treated by the courts as coming into this class. From about ten or eleven and upwards normal children are sufficiently intelligent to be sworn as ordinary witnesses, though judges and magistrates are always careful to question these young people first to make sure that they appreciate the responsibility of giving evidence and the importance of telling the truth when they do so.

Between this class and the very young is an intermediate class; a group whose ages range from, say, seven to eleven. Though they do not understand the nature of an oath, they may be sufficiently intelligent to give evidence and to understand the duty of telling the truth. In the case of children in this class, the law allows the courts to listen to their evidence but without putting them upon oath in criminal charges but not in civil cases. In civil proceedings if the child cannot be sworn his evidence cannot be received.

A quick practical test is to ask the child to read the oath and to express in his own words the meaning of what he has read. If he can come through these two tests well, he has provided the court with evidence both of his intelligence and of the possession of some sound elementary notions of ethics. Such a child can be allowed to be sworn as an ordinary witness. The evidence of a child who comes through the tests with less ease may be taken unsworn. Some children fail miserably in the 'reading test' but take a credit in 'morals'. These too may usually be allowed to give their evidence unsworn. Those who fail in both should in most cases not be heard at all.

The difference between the evidence of the child who can be sworn and the child who cannot is important. The court is entitled if it thinks fit to convict upon the evidence of the child who is sworn without the evidence of any other witness. The evidence of the child who is not sworn must be corroborated in a material particular by the evidence of another witness who has been sworn.

The last large group of incompetents is the 'husband and wife' class. The court must be particularly on its guard when asked by the prosecution to hear the evidence of one spouse against another when the latter happens to be the defendant to a criminal charge. The reason for this rule lies deep in the history of our common law. It would never allow a prisoner to convict himself 'out of his own mouth'. The prosecutor must prove his case and not expect the defendant to help him to do it for him. That is why as we saw in the last chapter the defendant to a criminal charge can be invited to set up a defence if he chooses but cannot be compelled to do so.

The immunity does not end with the defendant. It extends to his spouse. The common law like the Church regards husband and wife as one flesh, and to convict a man out of his wife's mouth is the same thing as to convict him out of his own mouth. If a husband is charged we must not allow his wife to give evidence against him. If a wife is charged we must not allow her husband to give evidence against her.

But into this old common law rule, Parliament has now made deep inroads. In a number of charges, one spouse may now give evidence against the other. The chief are charges of personal violence of one spouse upon another, bigamy, rape, abduction, carnal knowledge, incest, indecent assault, cruelty to children, obtaining benefit from the Labour Exchange by fraud, and charges of family neglect or abandonment under the Vagrancy Acts.

In the first of these charges, that is, a charge of personal violence of one spouse against another – attempted murder, for example – the spouse assaulted is not only competent but compellable. In all the others the wife, or husband as the case may be, cannot be compelled to give evidence. They are 'competent' but not 'compellable'. If a husband or wife is called to give evidence the clerk or chairman should first of all explain that he or she is not bound to give evidence against the accused spouse but may do so if he or she is willing.

Of course, these prohibitions apply only to the prosecution. The defendant is entitled in all cases to call his or her spouse as a witness for the defence.

Sometimes a witness is called to give evidence which may make him liable to criminal proceedings himself. For example, a person is charged with procuring abortion. The woman upon whom the abortion has been performed is called by the prosecution as a witness. She may appeal to the magistrates or the judge at the trial to be allowed to refuse to answer questions which may make her too liable to a charge of abortion.

Whether the protection is granted is a question for the court to decide, not for the witness. The appeal should be acceded to only where there is a real likelihood of the witness being later charged if compelled to make admissions in the witness box.

If a witness will not come voluntarily the magistrates have power to compel his attendance. The Magistrates' Courts Act, 1952, s. 77, allows them to summon any competent witness. The applicant – he may be the informant or defendant or a representative of either – must assert that the witness will not come without a summons and that he is likely to give material evidence on behalf of the person who wishes to call him. The summons must be served as are other summonses but cannot be sent by post and a reasonable sum must be left to cover the expense of attending court.

Should the witness summons be ignored a warrant may be issued on proof of the service of the summons. Where the applicant can satisfy the magistrate that it is probable that the witness will not appear upon a summons, a warrant may be issued without a preliminary witness summons if the proceedings are criminal but not if they are for a civil complaint. The warrant may be backed for bail and the applicant for it must be sworn.

If the witness refuses to give evidence, whether or not he has attended voluntarily, he may be sent to prison for as long as seven days 'or until he sooner gives evidence'.

Before giving evidence all witnesses except children whose testimony the court decides to hear unsworn must take the oath. The usual form is to swear to tell the truth 'by Almighty God', but witnesses for whom the taking of an oath is contrary to their religious belief, as for example Quakers, may affirm, and so may those who have no religious belief. Jewish witnesses are sworn on the Old Testament and Roman Catholics often ask for the Douay Bible. For a chance Moslem, the Koran should be at hand, whilst the Chinese bind themselves either by blowing out a candle or by breaking a saucer. The drama of extinction or destruction thus enacted in the eye of the Court, heightened by the suspense preceding it whilst the usher hurries in search of suitable properties, makes the oath of a Chinese the impressive and solemn ceremony it should be.

As far as possible a witness should be allowed to tell his own story. The common practice is to elicit his evidence by a series of questions which keep him to the points about which he is to speak. But whether these questions are put by the party who calls him or by his advocate or by the chairman or the clerk, they should never be 'leading'. They should never suggest the desired answer to the witness.

An amusing example of the leading question occurred some time ago when much depended upon the colour of a book.

'Was the colour of the book red?' asked learned counsel.

'A little leading, sir,' protested the chairman.

'Very well, your Worship,' replied the advocate indulgently, 'I will put the question in another way – This book, sir, was it or was it not – red?'

Both questions, of course, were leading inasmuch as they suggested the actual colour of the book. The proper question to have asked was, 'What was the colour of the book?'

After a witness has given evidence for the party who has called him, he may be questioned by the other side. This is called 'cross-examination' and is a right to which every prosecutor and defendant is entitled, though it is often wrongfully denied to a private prosecutor or to a police officer who may have brought the charge and is not represented by an advocate.

The cross-examiner is allowed a great deal of latitude. He may ask leading questions and he may ask questions about subjects of which the other side is not permitted to speak. A defendant, for example, may ask his accusers about his character. They may not volunteer this information unasked except in the few cases where an Act allows them to do so.

But to one limitation the cross-examiner is subject in the same way as the examiner in chief. His questions must be relevant to the charge the court is investigating, otherwise there would be no limit and a trial could be prolonged indefinitely.

After cross-examination the side calling the witness may question him again, but only upon points arising out of cross-examination and not to elicit evidence which was overlooked until the opponent's cross-examination brought it to mind.

Witnesses have not been treated well by the courts in the past. They have been bullied, mocked, threatened, and abused. Dickens' picture of Mr Winkle's encounter with Mr Justice Stareleigh was not merely funny. It was true, a commonplace of court practice in his day.

Often the witness has been made to bear the court's own shortcomings as the sins of Israel were laid upon the scapegoat. If the court was hard of hearing, he was accused of insufferable and deliberate mumbling. 'How could I have got Daniel on my notes unless you told me so, sir?' If the court through its own inattention or muddle-headedness failed to understand the witness, he would be lucky if he was accused of nothing worse than unreliability and might very well find himself hounded out of the witness box with the judge or chairman thundering that he left the court a discredited man.

Small wonder then that the first instinctive reaction of so many people when asked to say what they know about an incident which may lead to an appearance in court is to take refuge in an absence of mind which they hope will avoid a presence of body in the witness box.

To-day, however, the court which treats a witness rudely is very much the exception and not the rule. The only experience he has to fear is at a court where to his already onerous duties as magistrate the chairman has gratuitously added those of censor of dress. For such, 'a sweet disorder in the dress' has no charms. They yearn for a 'monstrous regiment of women', and of men too. A hatless female, a collarless male, will rouse them worse than a bad bit of perjury.

Once a witness came into court in beach pyjamas, twin pillars, the outward and visible sign as it were of feminine duplicity. They were, of course, hurried out of court to be exchanged for the regimental skirt. But what, we may ask, would have happened if their bold wearer had capped her impudence by refusing to give evidence except as she had originally appeared? Witnesses have a duty to give evidence, but magistrates have equally a duty to listen to them, and there is nothing in the Magistrates' Courts Act which says that a woman may not give evidence in trousers. An outraged chairman may, of course, consider a prosecution for indecency. Joan of Arc, it is true, was burnt amongst other things for wearing male bifurcated garments. But few courts would go so far as that to-day.

The wise bench interferes with a witness as little as possible, but carefully watches him. Manners maketh the witness and he should be allowed to comport himself as naturally as possible. If he wears an open shirt, if she has no hat, even if beach pyjama'd, it is best to say nothing but to make a mental note that this is the sort of person he or she is.

Not necessarily a bad sort either. It may be doubted whether the person who goes about comfortably dressed is more prone to perjury than those who attire themselves in honour of their appearance in court like tailor's dummies.

In closely contested cases often less depends on what a witness says than how he says it. At such a time a fussy consequentiousness serves a magistrate worst and a quiet self-effacement best. The good cricketer keeps his eye on the ball; the good magistrate keeps his eye on the witness; both say nothing.

Some time ago a most experienced magistrate had to try a charge in which a conviction meant also a finding of adultery against the defendant. He came to the conclusion that the allegations of the prosecution were true. A friend who read the evidence but had not been present at the trial commented that in view of the unshaken denials of the defendant he was surprised at the decision.

'She had,' replied the most experienced magistrate, 'a roving eye.'

CHAPTER 13

EVIDENCE

THIS chapter brings us to the third great restriction on judicial initiative. The law will not allow judges or magistrates to listen to a great many things upon which we commonly base our judgements in everyday life. In the last chapter we saw that it would not allow some persons to be called as witnesses at all. In this we shall see that those who may be called cannot tell the courts everything they may know.

Most of us pass judgement upon our fellow men too readily. It is a sobering practice to make a mental note for a few weeks of judgements we have made upon the actions of others which events have proved to be wrong. The law is well aware of this failing, and in arming its ministers with powers of condemnation and punishment it is also careful to see that they shall act upon only the best and most trustworthy evidence. The exclusion of all else – much of which outside the courts would be regarded as proof enough – often leads to acquittals so incomprehensible to many people that they assert with Mr Bumble that 'the law is a hass' when in truth it is almost always more charitable, more magnanimous and more just than its critics; much more than individuals is the law mindful of the apostolic behest 'In malice be children but in understanding be men'.

What is the best and most trustworthy evidence? The evidence of persons who have actually experienced with one or more of their own five senses something which tends to prove or disprove that the person accused has or has not committed an offence. All else must be excluded unless for special reasons the law of evidence will allow it to be given.

For example, White accuses Black of assaulting him. He calls Brown who says, 'I saw Black strike White.' This is admissible. Brown is giving evidence of what he actually saw himself. But if he says, 'Green told me that he saw

Black strike White,' this is not admissible because here Brown is only an intermediary. He was not the man on the spot. He is able to tell the court only what he has 'heard Green say' and such evidence is stigmatized as 'hearsay'. Brown may have misunderstood Green. Green may not have said it at all. So Brown must be sent away unheard and Green himself must be called. If he has indeed said that he saw Black strike White the court will now get it direct from him and will see with what assurance he says it and how he shapes when questioned by Black, and if need be will be able to remind him that he is on oath.

Or Brown may say, 'I didn't see the assault but Black's a nasty-looking beggar and in my opinion just the man to do it.' Such 'evidence' is constantly advanced in the street and market place, but in court it is rigorously excluded. The opinion of a witness is not evidence. Opinion is a conclusion drawn from facts, and this is for the magistrates to form. The witnesses present what they believe to be the facts. The magistrates come to their opinion upon them – another way of saying that they decide whether the defendant is guilty or not.

The opinion of experts upon matters which require special study or training, however, is admissible. White, for example, may have incurred a black eye and shown it to his doctor. The doctor can be called to give evidence about it, its severity, and whether the injury was consistent with a blow from a fist. A lawyer may be called to explain foreign law but not our own law which we are all presumed to know.

Upon a charge of cruelty to an animal, a veterinary surgeon may be called for the prosecution and another for the defence. These battles of the experts compensate the courts for many a tedious hour, and it is indeed diverting to watch two learned gentlemen setting out from the strained tendons of the same unassuming grey mare to reach conclusions as opposite as the poles.

Expert witnesses are not confined to doctors and veterinary surgeons and people of professional rank. The district nurse should be given a sympathetic hearing if it was to her and not to the local doctor that White took his damaged eye. An experienced constable may give evidence of drunkenness and a motorist of speed. A medical student may not be as skilled or experienced as a registered medical practitioner, but the court is entitled to hear his evidence and it is for the magistrates to decide to what extent they will rely upon it.

Or again Brown may say, 'I didn't see Black assault White but I know he assaulted Grey a month ago so I can quite believe he has assaulted White now.' A piece of information showing that Black had been guilty of similar acts and suggesting that he was rather prone to violence carries great weight in our everyday judgements, but the law will not allow its judges and magistrates to hear it unless the defendant by his own action gives to his accusers the right to call evidence about it.

The defendant may destroy his immunity in several ways – by asking the witnesses for the prosecution questions with a view to establishing his own good character; or by himself giving this evidence; or again, by giving evidence against any other person charged with the same offence.

He may also lose his immunity if he attacks the character of the witnesses for the prosecution and then himself gives evidence. If, however, he contents himself with attacking the witnesses but does not go into the witness box himself, the prosecution cannot give evidence of his bad character, because every defendant is entitled to show that the witnesses against him are untrustworthy (*R*. v. *Butterwasser* [1948], 1 K.B. 4).

Secondly, the defendant may destroy his immunity by his own conduct. Black for example may say, 'I did hit White but it was a pure accident.' In such circumstances White would be entitled to bring evidence to show that Black had had a similar accident with Grey or with Green. If the defendant sets up the defence of accident or mistake the prosecution is entitled to call witnesses to show that he has had similar accidents or has made similar mistakes in the past from which it may be reasonably concluded that his acts were not mistaken or unintentional but deliberate.

In a similar way evidence of other incidents or acts in addition to the one upon which a charge is based may be proved to show that the defendant was pursuing a deliberately planned system or course of conduct and was perfectly well aware of the criminal character of his actions.

This evidence of similar acts or conduct is tendered only upon charges in which the prosecution have to show that the defendant not only committed the act but also that he did it intentionally – as in the example we have taken of Black assaulting White or of one person taking another's umbrella. We find interesting examples of them in many famous criminal cases. Armstrong, it will be remembered, was accused of poisoning his wife. The prosecution was also allowed to show that between the death of Mrs Armstrong and the trial he had attempted to poison by similar means a rival solicitor. Armstrong had set up the defence that arsenic found in his possession had been purchased by him with the perfectly innocent intention of killing weeds. The evidence of the later attempt was admitted to show that his intention was not innocent at all but criminal.

In addition to this, there are a few charges upon which the prosecution is allowed to prove that the defendant has had a bad record no matter what defence he puts up. The best known of these is the charge of being 'a suspected person or reputed thief loitering with intent to commit a felony, contrary to the Vagrancy Act, 1824, s. 4'. The Prevention of Crimes Act, 1871, s. 15, says that such a defendant may be convicted 'if from the circumstances of the case and from his known character as proved to the court it appears that his intention was to commit a felony'.

CHAPTER 14

THE ATTITUDE OF THE ACCUSED

THIS chapter is really a continuation of the last, but its subject is of such importance that the break will serve to emphasize it.

A barrister who had defended many thousands of criminal cases used to say to solicitors who came to brief him, 'Don't tell me the evidence against your man. Tell me what he said when he was arrested.'

In reading the life of Sir Edward Marshall Hall it is astonishing to notice how often conviction or acquittal turned on the construction which that dominant man sought to persuade the jury to place on the prisoner's statements.

When spoken to of an alleged offence, an accused person will do one of two things. He may remain silent. Or he may reply to the accusation. Let us deal with the latter first.

The law regards statements of the defendant as of very great value as evidence – always provided they are made voluntarily; so great indeed that if when he presents himself at court and pleads guilty, no witnesses need be called and all that the bench has to consider is how to deal with the prisoner.

Apart from statements which may amount to a full confession, the defendant may make admissions which will be of the greatest assistance to the prosecutor in proving his case and to the court in indicating what defence the accused is setting up.

Thus to go back to the Black and White 'incident', Black may say, 'I struck him in self-defence,' when we shall see at once that the question is not whether Black struck White but whether White had acted in such a way as to justify Black in striking him.

But if Black says, 'I didn't strike him at all,' the court must address itself to the problem of whether in fact a blow was given.

An accused person too may make a number of conflicting statements or he may shift his ground when he realizes that his first story will not stand examination. Equivocation is often the ill-fitting cloak of the guilty mind.

But you may say, 'In Chapter 12 at page 77 you said that the common law would not allow a man to be convicted "out of his own mouth". How can you reconcile the admission of these statements with that?' The answer is that the extreme position taken up by the common law has been modified, partly by Parliament and partly by the judges, so that now statements made by an accused person or accounts of conversations between him and another person relevant to the charge are admissible as evidence always provided they are made voluntarily.

Before a witness can be allowed to give evidence of statements made by the accused the court must be assured that they were made of his own accord. If the prosecutor or the police in charge of the case have put any pressure upon him, as for example by threatening him or by coaxing an admission out of him, the statement is vitiated and cannot be admitted in evidence. It is for this reason that when a police officer gives evidence of a conversation he has had with the prisoner he will usually preface it with the statement that 'I cautioned the defendant and then said to him – ' or 'I charged the defendant and cautioned him and he then said – .' If the prosecutor or a witness does not mention the caution before giving evidence of a statement he alleges the defendant has made, he should be stopped and asked if a caution was administered and if not why not.

The caution usually is in this form, 'Do you wish to say anything in answer to the charge? You are not obliged to say anything unless you wish to do so, but whatever you say will be taken down in writing and may be given in evidence.'

Neither a police officer nor anyone else need administer a caution when making enquiries which may or may not lead to a charge being made. But the moment he has decided that there is sufficient evidence to justify a charge against a particular person, he should immediately be cautioned if it is proposed to question him further or to invite any statement from him.

Only persons connected with the charge and who are therefore in a position to threaten the accused or to promise him favourable treatment need administer the caution. Legally they are known as 'persons in authority' and examples of them are the prosecutor himself, the police, and magistrates dealing with the case. An employer is not a 'person in authority' unless he is also the prosecutor or closely interested in the case.

Although statements obtained by threat or promise are not admissible, evidence of what has been discovered as a consequence of those statements may be given. There is an amusing case of a man who was charged with stealing a lantern. The police by threats induced him to say that he threw the lantern into a pond. This statement was of course inadmissible. But the pond was dragged, the lantern brought to the surface and the fact that it was so found was allowed to be given in evidence (*R.* v. *Gould* (1840), 9 C. & P. 364).

But what if the defendant when accused remains silent? In everyday life we say 'Silence gives consent'. If an innocent person is accused of a crime we expect as a matter of course a prompt denial if not some explanation. So does the law, but not after the prosecutor or the police have made up their minds to charge and caution him. The whole purpose of the caution is to inform him of his right to be silent. He is entitled to exercise that right and leave to the prosecution the task of proving his guilt.

Let us illustrate this with two cases actually decided by the judges. The first is *R.* v. *Marks Feigenbaum* [1919], 1 K.B. 431. Feigenbaum was charged with inciting boys to steal fodder. The boys were arrested for the theft and said that Feigenbaum had incited them to commit the crime. Naturally a police officer went off to tell Feigenbaum about these allegations but to them he answered never a word. The judges held that the prosecution could make this silence part of their case against him.

Suppose, however, that the police officer had gone to Feigenbaum with his mind made up to charge him and had for that reason administered a caution. The prosecution then could not have set up as part of its case the fact that the defendant had made no reply.

This is just what happened in the case of *R.* v. *Whitehead* [1929], 1 K.B. 99; 92 J.P. 197. The defendant here was charged with an offence against a girl under sixteen. He was charged by a police officer and given the usual warning that he need not say anything in answer to the charge unless he wished to do so but that, if he did say anything, whatever he said would be taken down in writing and given in evidence. To this he made no reply.

The judge at the trial directed the jury that the defendant's silence could be regarded as corroboration of the girl's story. But the Court of Criminal Appeal held that this was a misdirection. Lord Alverstone's judgement in an earlier case was quoted with approval when he said: 'The non-denial of the offence by the prisoner when finally charged by the police is not corroboration. We are far from saying that evidence of non-denial cannot be corroboration, for in some cases the absence of indignant denial would be; but non-denial of a formal charge made by the police is not, or may not be, on the same footing.'

Sometimes accusations are made by writing – usually by letter. In no circumstances can the failure to answer a written accusation be treated as evidence of the admission of guilt. To the contention that it could, here is the robust retort of Lord Esher, a former Master of the Rolls.

'Where merchants are in dispute one with the other in the course of carrying on some business negotiations, and one writes to the other, "but you promised me that you would do this or that", if the other does not answer the letter, but proceeds with the negotiations, he must be taken to admit the truth of the statement. But such cases are wholly unlike the case of a letter charging a man with some offence or meanness. Is it the ordinary habit of mankind, of which the courts will take notice, to answer such letters; and must it be taken, according to the ordinary practice of mankind, that if a man does not answer he admits the truth of the charge made against him? If it were so, life would be unbearable. A man might day by day write such letters, which, if they are not answered, would be brought forward as evidence of the truth of the charges made in them. The ordinary and wise practice is not to answer them – to take no notice of them' (*Wiedemann* v. *Walpole* [1891], 2 Q.B. 534).

So much for the attitude of the accused. What of the attitude of the court? Here we must keep clearly in mind what is the object of the rules we have just been considering and what is not. Their object is to prevent a prosecutor from obtaining admissions from a defendant by duress, by fraud, or by promises; by what used to be stigmatized as Star Chamber methods and is to-day called 'third degree'. But their object is not to place a man who gives a frank explanation of his actions at the outset upon the same footing as one who like Brer Fox 'lies low and sez nothing'.

When at last the jury at Assizes or Quarter Sessions or the magistrates in a summary court have to decide whether the accused is guilty or not guilty, the attitude of the defendant is a factor which they must take into consideration. A defendant may have given an explanation of his conduct which is difficult to believe, but if he gives it at once when challenged and sticks to it unshaken throughout the proceedings, that explanation for all its incredibility may achieve his acquittal when a more plausible explanation kept back until the trial may fail; for the jury and magistrates are entitled to ask themselves: 'If this man had such a good answer to the charge why did he not bring it out before?' Whilst if he makes no reply at all conviction must follow as the night the day if the court finds that the prosecutor has set up a case to answer.

CHAPTER 15

BEHIND THE DEFENDANT'S BACK

In criminal charges – and indeed in civil complaints too – most of the evidence is either of acts committed by the prisoner or in his presence; or of conversations with him or which have taken place in his hearing.

As a general rule a person is held responsible neither inside the courts nor outside for what happens behind his back, but there are important exceptions to this rule. To begin with, the courts are not limited to evidence of what has taken place when the defendant is present if the evidence of other facts is needed to give a complete picture of what it is alleged he has done.

Thus, Black may be charged with stealing a parcel from a railway platform. In addition to proving that he was seen to take the parcel, the prosecutor must show that it belonged to someone else and not to Black. To do this he must call witnesses who can say to whom the parcel belonged and to identify it and to show how it came to be on the platform. It is highly unlikely that any of these witnesses will have ever seen the defendant before or that any of the transactions of which they speak were done in his presence. But their evidence is admissible to prove certain elements of the charge – that the prisoner did not own the parcel and that he took it without permission whilst it was in the care of the railway.

Conversations which have taken place in the absence of the prisoner are admitted far less readily. If evidence of an act is admissible then a statement made at the time the act was committed and forming part of it is also admissible, though the defendant was not present and could not hear what was said. Instances rarely occur where this rule applies, and the statement can be admitted only if it actually accompanies the act, not if made after its accomplishment.

Here is a case where such a statement was admitted. A man was shot. In the room with him was another man. Just before the shot was fired this man looked up and said, 'There's Butcher' – 'Butcher' being the defendant. The exclamation was regarded as an inseparable part of the act of looking up and the recognition of the prisoner. It was admitted though not made in the presence of the prisoner.

Let us contrast this with another very similar case, but in which a similar exclamation was rejected. A man cut a woman's throat. She ran out of the house exclaiming, 'Oh, aunt, see what A. has done to me.' It was held that this statement was inadmissible because it was made after the act had been completed.

These two cases show how carefully such statements made in the absence of the accused are scrutinized before they are admitted. Generally if there is any doubt about such a statement being really part of an act committed in the absence of the prisoner, it is better to rule it out.

In certain charges the general rule has been relaxed where to shut out the evidence of such conversations would favour the accused to an unfair degree. The most important of these relaxations is the 'dying declaration'. It is admissible only in charges of murder and manslaughter. In many cases the victim is the only witness of the defendant's act. If his statement of how he was done to death were shut out because his assailant was not present to hear it, this would greatly favour the homicide. And so very properly the dying declaration has been made an exception to the general rule, but before the court can accept the evidence of such a declaration it must be assured that the declarant realized that he was dying and had no hope of recovery.

The dying declaration is the most striking as well as the most complete exception to the rule of hearsay – the rule which as we saw in Chapter 13 insists that only the person who actually sensed the commission of an act may be called as a witness, and not a person to whom he told what he had experienced. The witness to a dying declaration reports what the dying person has told him. If the court considers that witness trustworthy they may treat the allegations made in the declaration as proof of facts needed to establish the charge, although it was not made on oath.

The reason for this great breach in the rule of hearsay has been impressively stated by a judge. 'The general principle on which this species of evidence is admitted,' he said, 'is that they are declarations made in extremity when the party is at the point of death, and when every hope of this world is gone; when every motive to falsehood is silenced, and the mind is induced by the most powerful considerations to speak the truth; a situation so solemn and so awful is considered by law as creating an obligation equal to that imposed by a positive oath administered in a court of justice' (*R.* v. *Woodcock* (1789), 1 Leach C.C. 500).

Death need not be immediate, but the declarant must feel it to be imminent and inevitable. There is no need to tell him he is dying. He need make no statement about his condition provided evidence is forthcoming which convinces the court that from his demeanour he had abandoned all hope of recovery. Any competent person can be called as a witness of such a declaration. Many people think that only a magistrate can hear it. They confuse the dying declaration with the power of a magistrate to take the deposition of a sick person which may be read in his absence at a trial at Assizes or Quarter Sessions if the invalid witness is unable to attend personally. This is dealt with in Chapter 29.

A complaint made by a woman who has been raped is also admissible though not made in the presence of the man she accuses. It is admitted not to prove that what she says is true but to show that the assault committed upon her was done against her will and that in making the complaint she had acted as we should expect a woman who had been outraged in this way would behave.

The complaint is admissible only if made at the earliest possible moment after the assault to a person to whom we should expect the woman to make such a complaint – to a relative or friend, for example, or to a constable.

The rule in charges of rape has been gradually extended

until now it covers all charges of indecent assault, such as indecent assault upon girls, indecency with boys, and sodomy.

Finally where two or more persons are charged with conspiracy anything said or done by one of them in furtherance of the conspiracy is admissible in evidence against the others though they may not have been present when the statements were made or the acts committed.

There are, of course, other instances where evidence of what has occurred 'behind the defendant's back' is admissible, but they arise only rarely and cannot be included here.

CHAPTER 16

BEYOND REASONABLE DOUBT

WE come to the last and greatest restriction on judicial initiative. Judges and magistrates must not convict a person of a criminal offence unless the evidence against him proves his guilt 'beyond reasonable doubt'.

Not only is this the greatest of the restrictions we have been considering. It is also certainly the most difficult to describe and apply. We may take care never to allow an incompetent witness to give evidence or a competent witness to say what he should not. But for reasonable doubt we need an explorer's flair. It is an ill-defined territory the boundaries of which must be rediscovered for every contested charge. It lies between certainty and uncertainty, hard by the realms of probability. The definition of its limits often varies as much with the personnel of the bench as with the circumstances of the charge. Some intrepid spirits will consider the evidence has taken them well beyond the fateful boundary when others will feel they have never glimpsed it.

The question is one which each individual magistrate must decide for himself. If he is inclined to acquit when his brethren would convict, he should explain his doubts before he allows them to overrule him.

Particularly must he be on his guard against any movement to side-track the issue. The problem is, 'Has the prosecutor proved the guilt of the person he is accusing beyond reasonable doubt?' The answer to that question is not, 'Well, we are going to put him on probation so it won't do him any harm and may do him a lot of good'; nor 'There's been too much of this sort of thing lately and we must put a stop to it'; nor 'We must back up the police'; nor 'The young man who is prosecuting is such a nice young fellow.'

Considerations like these insinuate themselves or are

passed round in undertones from one magistrate to another whenever the bench is faced with a difficult charge to decide. They are the expression of the English love of compromise which seeks so hopefully to find a solution 'satisfactory to all parties'. Unfortunately, this is one instance where no compromise is possible.

The meaning of the term was explained with great lucidity by Lord Hewart in his address to the jury at the trial of William Podmore for murder.

'You have been reminded,' said His Lordship, 'and rightly reminded that the burden of proof in such a prosecution, as indeed in nearly all prosecutions, is upon those who make the charge. The prisoner is not required to prove his innocence. What is required, if conviction there is to be, is that those who are responsible for the prosecution, shall, as a result of the evidence, considered as a whole, establish that guilt beyond reasonable doubt. You will not, I am sure, allow yourselves to be bewildered or troubled by such a phrase. What it means is not some whimsical or fanciful doubt, which a person might conjure up for the purpose of creating a difficulty, but such a doubt as would govern a man's course of action in some private affair of moment of his own. Unless you are satisfied beyond a doubt of that kind that the accused person is guilty, then he is entitled to be acquitted.'

This is how Mr Justice Darling explained the term in his address to the jury in the Armstrong case:

'A reasonable doubt means this: it does not mean that you do not like to do it, it does not mean that it is disagreeable to you, it does not mean that by some possible hypothesis you can arrive at that conclusion. There is hardly anything of which a really subtle and ingenious mind cannot convince itself; there is hardly any truth that a subtle and ingenious person cannot bring himself honestly to doubt. But it means that you say you are convinced, unless when you consider the facts, you have a reasonable doubt as to whether the matter is proved or whether it is not, a reasonable doubt in

MC—4

this sense. If it is the kind of doubt, not such as you would conjure up in the middle of the night, but such a reasonable doubt as in the daytime when you are about your business would lead you to say, "Well, I cannot make up my mind about it." '

Mr Justice Darling was addressing a jury of countrymen, and he went on to give this homely illustration:

'Suppose you were buying a horse or selling one, and you had to resolve suddenly whether he had got some disease, say, spavin. You say, "I am not sure he has, maybe he has not, but it is so uncertain that I cannot say one way or the other." That would be a reasonable doubt' (*R.* v. *Armstrong* [1922], 2 K.B. 555; 86 J.P. 209).

The magistrates have not to be able to say, 'We are certain he did it.' They must be able to say more than 'He probably did it.' Perhaps 'No reasonable man could doubt he did it' most nearly expresses the standard needed. If all the members of the bench so express themselves, then in those contested charges where the question of reasonable doubt arises in an acute form they are not likely to convict the innocent or acquit the guilty.

One generalization may be permitted. If the accused has survived the shocks of accusation and trial, has gone into the witness box and faced cross-examination without making some damning admission or telling some palpable falsehood, then surely there is doubt. If going further he throws into the balance a character which the prosecution cannot impeach, then not only is there doubt, but to convict is to run a real risk of a miscarriage of justice. The law does not ask its servants to run that risk.

Admittedly the defendant's denials may be the most brazen impudence. But they may be true. And 'there's the rub', to quote Hamlet, whose tragedy is popularly thought to be a tragedy of irresolution but which is really much more. It is the drama of a highly judicial mind wrestling with doubt.

Hamlet suspects that his uncle and his mother have murdered his father, the late King of Denmark, to usurp his throne. His father's ghost appears before him upon the battlements of Elsinore. He tells Hamlet not only that he was murdered but how – the usurping uncle poured poison into his ear whilst he slept. 'O my prophetic soul,' shouts Hamlet, but later he reflects 'The spirit that I have seen May be the devil . . . yea, and perhaps . . . Abuses me to damn me.'

'I'll have grounds more relative than this,' he says, and to resolve his doubts he devises a test 'wherein I'll catch the conscience of the King.' He stages a play witnessed by his uncle and mother and the court. In the play a stage king is murdered in precisely the same way as the ghost has described his own murder. Hamlet's uncle and mother suspecting that their crime is discovered are seized with panic. They rush from the room leaving the play unfinished. The stratagem has taken the matter beyond the realms of reasonable doubt. 'I'll take the ghost's word for a thousand pound,' cries Hamlet.

To-day as never before courts are far more than mere depositories to punish. In very truth they hold the destinies of their fellow men they are called upon to try in the hollow of their hand. In his 'Elegy' Gray writes: 'Each in his narrow cell for ever laid, The rude forefathers of the hamlet sleep.' In our own day standardization is tending to place us in our cell long before we pass through the churchyard gates for the last time. With our niche we are given great privileges, a firm and abiding social status, regular salaries, calculable increments, holidays, the expectation of promotion, benefits in sickness, pensions in old age. But make one step without the bounds of probity – the taking of a paltry half crown; a moment of irresponsibility; a sudden inexplicable, uncontrollable gesture, and all can come tumbling about our ears.

Magistrates and judges are often the arbiters as to whether that one false step has been taken and whether in consequence all the rights and privileges so patiently acquired in the passing years are forfeit. The contemplation of such responsibility is one that must give the boldest pause.

Some years ago a young schoolmaster was accused by a

nursemaid of indecently assaulting her. After a careful hearing he was convicted by a summary court. He appealed. Quarter Sessions upheld the decision. With conviction everything that the young man had acquired was lost. The short sentence of imprisonment imposed was the least of his troubles. His reputation was gone. All the years he had spent in qualifying for his position were wasted. Place, promotion, privileges, rights, all went and with it the faith and love of his wife, his children, his friends. Irreparable ruin followed the decision of the two courts.

Some time later the nursemaid entered a hospital. She had not been there long before she was accusing doctors and medical students of indecently assaulting her. The girl was demented. She thought every man who came near her committed this criminal act. Happily someone thought of the young schoolmaster, and as far as it was possible to do so he was rehabilitated.

This is not an isolated case. Read the extraordinary case of Adolf Beck and those summarized in that most entertaining of criminal works 'Wills on Circumstantial Evidence' and you will see how wary we must be if circumstances are not to make fools of us all.

CHAPTER 17

GUILTY OR NOT GUILTY

Now comes the moment when the court must decide whether the defendant is guilty or not guilty.

Unlike a jury, the magistrates need not be unanimous. A majority one way or the other is sufficient. If they disagree and both sides are equal in number, they may adjourn the case to another day to be heard by a differently constituted bench. But if there is disagreement upon this proposition also, then the defendant must be acquitted.

The chairman votes with the rest of his colleagues. He has no casting vote.

If the verdict is not guilty, the defendant is 'dismissed'. The finding is entered in the court register, and after it has been recorded the defendant cannot be charged with the same offence again; no matter if, as he sometimes does, immediately upon getting into the street, he proclaims his guilt to the housetops. 'No one,' says an age-honoured maxim, 'shall be vexed with the same accusation twice.'

If, on the other hand, the defendant is found guilty, then the court will pass on to the anxious task of devising a punishment to fit the crime; or – since reformation now plays so great a part in the decisions of the criminal courts – of prescribing a treatment calculated to remedy the defendant's anti-social conduct.

CHAPTER 18

DETERMINING THE SENTENCE

WRITERS on crime and punishment commonly liken justices determining a fit sentence for the punishment of a crime to a doctor making up a prescription. If there were any truth in the image no better argument could be found for the immediate abolition of the lay magistracy. An amateur is no fit person to be mixing drugs and poisons whether they be real or metaphorical.

The image is not a true one. So great are the permutations and combinations into which modern drugs can be made up that a doctor might write a different prescription for every patient he treats in the practice of a lifetime and yet not write two alike. Magistrates have no such range. At most they can do only four things. They can generally fine their man. They can often imprison him. They can always place him on probation, and they can make him find sureties to keep the peace. Occasionally they may see fit to combine some of these punishments.

Moreover provided he keeps a weather eye open for the Coroner, the medical man is free to try out any drug he likes upon a patient. The courts enjoy no such freedom. There are standards of sentence to which all courts in varying degree conform. Criminal charges to-day are dealt with in certain well marked ways. What passed as a fit sentence a hundred, fifty, even twenty years ago would almost certainly now raise a storm of protest. The courts of 1950 have much the same powers as they had in 1900. But they do not exercise them in the same way. They dare not. The standard has changed. Unseen, written in no law book, it is there as real to judges and justices as is our unwritten constitution to our statesmen and the bench which would flout it is riding sooner or later for a fall.

Ask a barrister with some experience at the criminal bar what would be done with a young man of hitherto good character convicted of forging a cheque of his employers for, say, £90. Few would say as much as six months' imprisonment – some would suggest probation. In Galsworthy's *Justice* you will find just such a young man convicted of just such an offence. Galsworthy's judge sentences William Falder to three years' penal servitude. 'Too much,' you say, and so it would be for to-day, but not for 1910 when the play was written. Indeed before determining the sentence Galsworthy canvassed judges and barristers amongst his friends and they agreed that three years' penal servitude was about the right sentence. Since then our attitude has changed. To-day we should regard such a sentence as intolerably severe and should confidently expect the Court of Criminal Appeal to reduce it. On the other hand, in 1800 Falder would have been lucky to have escaped hanging.

The law itself fixes a rough standard by setting a limit to the maximum penalties a court can impose. For the great majority of summary offences only a fine can be imposed in the first instance and where imprisonment without the option of a fine can be inflicted the sentence can rarely exceed six months.

For minor offences most courts have their own tariff of fines varying from ten shillings to five pounds according to the character of the particular breach, the means of the defendant, his past record, and his patience and resignation when called to book by authority.

But further than this we can detect a standard of treatment, not perhaps so clearly marked, admittedly with many notable exceptions, but nevertheless a standard all the same, in the way the more serious charges are dealt with – that is to say, assaults, offences against the Vagrancy Acts, and that great class of Indictable Offences which may be dealt with summarily – stealing, false pretences, embezzlement, and the like.

Varied as are the benches which sit in different parts of the country, in town and village, in the industrial north, and in the agricultural south, we shall find that they all conform to unwritten and yet generally accepted practices of dealing with delinquents they find guilty. So much so that if you give an experienced magistrate or clerk the salient facts of a case – the charge, the prisoner's age and sex, and previous convictions, if any – he will predict the court's decision with surprising accuracy.

Thus it almost amounts to a rule of practice to-day that a person dealt with in the summary courts is not sent to prison if it is the first time he has been found guilty. There are plenty of exceptions to the rule, of course; as, for example, where a defendant refuses to fall in with any provisions the court may think it desirable to make in the hope of reforming him and so preventing any further breaches of the law; or again where an epidemic of a particular kind of crime has broken out, such as thieving from the docks or shoplifting; or where a defendant though charged for the first time has in fact committed a series of crimes before being detected, such as a clerk embezzling his employer's money over a period; or again where he has carried out the crime with craft and premeditation. But in spite of these exceptions, the general rule holds good – a first offender is not sentenced to imprisonment for any crime unless there are circumstances which seriously increase the gravity of the offence.

A second general rule of practice is that youthful delinquents are not sent to prison even if found guilty a second or third time. Up to an age varying from 21 to 25 the courts are becoming more and more anxious to avoid sending a delinquent to prison and persevere with the reformatory powers they have at their command. Occasionally, of course, they are confronted with a young person who will respond to no efforts to reclaim him and for whom imprisonment is the only treatment.

Finally, imprisonment is being more and more regarded as a last resort whatever the age of the convicted person. It is inflicted only in those cases where any other form of treatment would be regarded as inadequate.

It is not a corollary from the rules of practice we have

just described that anyone who has once been sent to prison will go on being sent to prison for any subsequent offences of which he may be convicted. Quite often of course when once a delinquent appears to have set off upon a criminal career imprisonment follows each succeeding conviction with monotonous regularity. Happily there are many exceptions. Courts are often bold enough to try probation or a fine even in these cases, especially where the conviction occurs long years after others or is for a trivial offence.

You may say, 'Oh, but the determination of sentence is such an individual matter. Every case is different. Every bench dealing with it is different. Every offender is different. You cannot reduce the whole art of dealing with criminals to three rules.'

If you think this, cut out the next hundred cases reported at length in the press of serious charges dealt with before magistrates. You will be surprised to find how many of them fall into line with the three rules of practice set out in this Chapter.

Or take the criminal statistics. According to the criminal statistics for 1938 of offenders found guilty by the magistrates of committing an indictable offence (Table IX), only twenty-two in a hundred were sent to prison. Of these twenty-two we may be sure a good proportion had been previously found guilty of offences and that the remainder had some exceptional feature. In the 'Introductory Note' at page 14 we are told that the number of young persons under twenty-one years of age sent to prison for indictable offences was 702. The number of young persons under twenty-one found guilty of indictable offences was 37,322 (page 12); so that only one in fifty was sent to prison.

Some magistrates will complain, 'These rules do perhaps superficially outline our practice but we put a great deal more than this into the determination of the proper punishment. We study a case psychologically, for example – medically – socially – historically.' No doubt, and no attempt is made here to belittle such investigations but, however thorough a bench may be, it will be found that the rules described apply to them as to others, except probably that they use the Probation of Offenders Acts more often.

Or a dominant Chairman may say, 'A fig for your rules, Sir Nobody. Who made thee a lawgiver in Israel? I am not to be circumscribed by what is done at other courts. I have a discretion. I am upon the bench because I am I. I am here to administer the law as I think proper. You tell me that at all courts – practically all, anyway – a crook can count on getting away with nothing worse than probation the first time he's caught. No wonder this larceny business is still going on. The trouble is we've put up with it too long. The Romans were bothered with it. Even Moses. I'm going to stop it. Every thief I convict goes to prison for a month.'

There is nothing in law to stop a magistrate who embarks on this course. But it will be surprising if his path is not full of obstacles. His fellow justices may be 'First conviction – probation' men. They may object to his month. He can do nothing without them.

But possibly his personality is strong enough to carry his colleagues with him. They agree to send every thief down for a month. What will happen? Within a few weeks every solicitor practising at the court will be determined never to let it deal with a charge of larceny again. For it will be remembered, as we saw in Chapter 8, that a charge of larceny can be dealt with summarily only if the defendant consents. Other defendants who appear without an advocate will have friends in the know who will give them the tip to elect for Quarter Sessions and the jury. To the magistrates will be left the friendless and the poor and even some of these will escape them by contriving to appeal. Then the press may get difficult. The contrast between the sentences of this court and those of neighbouring benches will be too good to be missed. Assuredly it will not be missed. For all this a determined magistrate may go on undaunted. But he must not be surprised if his colleagues falter. The path of non-conformity is never easy or popular.

This tendency towards standardization of sentence is surely a desirable trend. Individual benches should subordinate their own inclinations to the general practice. They are all ministers deputizing for the Blind Goddess from whom we expect not only impartiality but even-handedness, an attribute much more difficult to attain in a large community like ours where she has to delegate her powers to all sorts and conditions of men and women. We expect her to treat us all alike, and this cannot be achieved if every magistrate takes his own line and 'gangs his own gait'.

That this trend has the support of the community is clearly shown in the Criminal Justice Act, 1948. The new Act is the lineal descendant of a succession of liberal measures designed to reduce the number of persons sent to prison as far as is compatible with social security. In the past the Legislature has been content with suggesting means by which the Courts may deal with delinquents in other ways such as probation and training centres. The new Act has done with counsel and persuasion. It actually prohibits the imposition of sentences of imprisonment upon certain classes of offenders as we shall see in Chapter 21.

CHAPTER 19

FINES

MOST summary offences can be punished only by the imposition of a fine, though a distress warrant or imprisonment may follow if it is not paid.

How great a fine magistrates are permitted to impose is to be found in the Act or Acts creating the offence. In some the section which describes the offence also tells us how it is to be treated. Thus turning up *Stone* under 'Pedlars' we shall find that to act as a pedlar without a certificate the maximum penalty is ten shillings for the first offence and twenty for a subsequent. The section says nothing about imprisonment and so we know the magistrates have no power to imprison anyone for this offence except those who have been fined and who have failed to pay.

Large modern Acts of Parliament often have a general 'penalty section' telling us how an act declared in the preceding sections to be an 'offence' is to be punished. To take once again the Road Traffic Act, 1930, as an example, 'driving without due care and attention' under Section 12 is described as 'an offence'. Turning on to Section 113 (2) we find that 'A person guilty of an offence under this Act for which no special penalty is provided shall be liable in the case of the first offence to a fine not exceeding twenty pounds.'

A number of the more serious offences created by these Acts are lifted out of the ordinary run to mark their graver character by allowing the courts to impose higher fines upon conviction for them and in some cases even imprisonment without the option of a fine. In all these cases we shall find that the punishment is set out in the section creating the offence. Thus, Section 11, the Dangerous Driving Section of the Road Traffic Act, permits a fine of 'not exceeding fifty pounds' for a first offence and a hundred for the second.

The amount of fines imposed for common offences varies a great deal with each court. Usually there is a rough scale determined by the magistrates in advance which is applied to each individual case. Modern Acts are much more generous in the maximum fines they allow courts of summary jurisdiction to impose – usually twenty pounds, when in Victorian days it was often no more than a niggardly forty shillings. The fines actually imposed, however, rarely approach the maximum permitted closely unless the circumstances of a particular offence make it an unusually bad one.

Until the Criminal Justice Act, 1948, became law the Judge at Assizes and the Chairman of Quarter Sessions had no power to impose a fine for felony, but the magistrates dealing summarily with any offence never laboured under a similar restriction. The fine is often a useful compromise between imprisonment and dismissal under the Probation of Offenders Acts. It is often most effective as a means of bringing home to delinquents the uneconomic character of evil doing; or in the homelier words of an experienced Justice, 'To make 'em see it don't pay.' Addressing a defendant who had helped himself in a butcher's shop, this same worthy observed trenchantly, 'I'll make this a very dear leg of pork for you, my friend.'

If the sum adjudged to be paid, which may include costs and compensation, is not paid, distress may be levied on the defaulter's goods; or without attempting a distraint, he may be sent to prison. The length of imprisonment depends upon the amount the defendant has been adjudged to pay. The scale is determined by the Magistrates' Courts Act, 1952, Third Schedule, and is as follows:

Amount not exceeding 10s, imprisonment must not exceed 7 days.

Amount not exceeding £1, imprisonment must not exceed 14 days.

Amount not exceeding £5, imprisonment must not exceed 1 month.

Amount not exceeding £20, imprisonment must not exceed 2 months.

Amount exceeds £20, imprisonment must not exceed 3 months.

The magistrates are not bound to impose the full imprisonment which a fine will carry. On the other hand there is a minimum alternative of five days.

The term 'fine' is not a euphemism for imprisonment. Parliament in deciding that an offence shall be punishable by fine intends that every reasonable chance shall be given to the defendant to pay it. If there were any doubt about this, a series of Acts of Parliament could be cited to prove it.

As long ago as 1879 the Summary Jurisdiction Act of that year empowered the courts to accept instalments of fines. This power is preserved in Section 63 (1) of the Magistrates' Courts Acts, 1952, though even to-day courts are to be found which pay scant attention to the section. Many working men can put aside two or three shillings per week when they cannot accumulate the total sum needed. It is surely sound economics to take these instalments. Six, even a dozen, extra entries in the court account books are much cheaper than keeping a man idle behind prison walls for a week or a fortnight whilst employing two or three others to look after him during the time he is there.

The Criminal Justice Administration Act, 1914, went further. It not only allowed magistrates to give defendants time to pay their fines. It compelled them to do so unless the defaulter was able to pay at once, or did not want the time, or had no fixed abode at which he could be found should he eventually fail to pay.

The same Act directed the magistrates when fixing the amount of any fine to be imposed on an offender to 'take into consideration, amongst other things, the means of the offender so far as they appear or are known to the court'. A chauffeur, for instance, should be fined appreciably less than a wealthy employer if both have committed similar offences. On the other hand if the chauffeur's offence is much more serious in character than the employer's a fine imposed upon the servant may be quite properly much higher than

the master's. The court has primarily to decide the adequate
penalty for the punishment of an offence and not how much
a convicted person can conveniently afford to pay out of
whatever happens to be his income.

The Money Payments (Justices Procedure) Act, 1935,
went further still. To ensure that the defendant had every
opportunity to pay his fine, it directed that magistrates
should not enter in their register the alternative imprisonment where they imposed a fine unless the defendant is
present and they had some special reason for doing so – such
as 'the gravity of the offence, the character of the defendant,
or other special circumstances.' If the fine is not paid the
imprisonment in default is to be decided later after a
summons has been issued requiring the defendant to attend
court to explain his default. In their discretion instead of
issuing a summons the magistrates may issue a warrant. If
when he appears the defaulter can give satisfactory reasons
for his failure, the magistrates can allow him further time.
If not they can then but not until then fix the alternative.

The innovation was a valuable one because it sets up a
special enquiry at which the court's attention is focused on
one question and one question only – has everything been
done to give the defaulter the chance of getting the money
together?

Another excellent provision of the same Act allowed the
magistrates to place a person who has been fined under the
supervision of a probation officer or some other suitable
person. Where the defaulter is under twenty-one he must
be placed under supervision unless the magistrates think it
would be impracticable or undesirable to do so.

All these provisions have been preserved in the Magistrates' Courts Act, 1952, Sections 63 to 72. If, after they have
been complied with, the fine still remains unpaid, the alternative must be imposed, but only if the court finds that the
defendant has had the means to pay the fine and could have
done so had he wished.

This is the effect of the judges' interpretation upon the

Act (*R.* v. *Woking Justices*, ex parte *Johnstone* [1942], 2 K.B. 248) though it is probably safe to say that when it was passed the draughtsmen did not think that this interpretation would be placed upon it. They thought the courts would be able to fix an alternative sentence of imprisonment irrespective of the means of the defendant just as they would if they had fixed the alternative at the same time as when the fine was imposed.

The decision is an unfortunate one because many courts in order to avoid this consequence make a practice of fixing an alternative despite the directions of Section 69 of the Magistrates' Courts Act, alleging that they do so because of the 'gravity of the offence'.

The result of this series of restrictions on the magistrates' powers to order immediate imprisonment if a fine is not paid is shown in the statistics. For the years 1909 to 1913 the average number of committals for non-payment of fines was 83,187 each year. In 1933 the number had fallen to 11,615. After the passing of the Money Payments (Justices Procedure) Act, 1935, the number fell again in 1944 to less than 4,000.

This is surely a worth-while achievement, for most people are now agreed that the ill consequences of short prison sentences of a few weeks are often out of all proportion to the evil they are intended to punish. An enforced absence of seven to fourteen days, for example, may mean that a man loses his employment, with disastrous results for himself, his family, and last but not least the community itself which ordained it.

CHAPTER 20

IMPRISONMENT

As for fines, whether magistrates are entitled to sentence a person to imprisonment depends upon an Act of Parliament, sometimes upon a combination of Acts of Parliament.

In non-indictable offences if this power is given we shall find it in the Act or Acts creating the offence. Thus turning again to the Road Traffic Act, we shall find Section 11 allows the summary courts to impose a sentence of four months in the first instance upon any person convicted of dangerous driving. If, however, we turn back to the Pedlars Act we shall find that Section 2 says nothing about imprisonment for a man convicted of acting as a pedlar without a certificate, and from this we conclude that such an offence cannot be punished by imprisonment 'without the option'.

For indictable offences dealt with summarily as explained in Chapter 8 we do not have to look to individual Acts for authority to imprison in the first instance. This is contained in the Magistrates' Courts Act, 1952, Section 19, and the maximum sentence is six months for each offence.

Sentences of imprisonment may be concurrent or consecutive. Here again it is important to bear in mind the distinction between indictable offences and non-indictable offences. If a person is convicted of two or more indictable offences dealt with summarily, he may be imprisoned for each for a maximum of six months to run consecutively, but the combined sentences must not amount to more than twelve months in all. If a person is convicted of two or more non-indictable offences, he may be sentenced to imprisonment for each to run consecutively, but the maximum imprisonment must not exceed six months.

Suppose, for example, a defendant is convicted of assaulting a police officer. This is a summary offence for which the maximum is six months. Suppose too that he is also convicted summarily of stealing the constable's whistle. Here

again the maximum is six months. But as there is only one
indictable offence the maximum imprisonment for both
offences cannot exceed six months.

Suppose, however, that the same defendant is convicted
of yet another offence of stealing. He would then be convicted of two indictable offences and the magistrates could
arrange their sentences for these offences to run consecutively, subject to the limitation of twelve months.

In many cases the magistrates are permitted to impose
both a fine and imprisonment. Thus for every indictable
offence tried summarily they may impose a fine of £100 and
send the defendant to prison for six months. In such a case
where the defendant fails to pay the fine he may be sent to
prison for upwards of three months in default and the magistrates may order this term to begin at the expiration of the
sentence of imprisonment for the same offence.

Thus, for example, a defendant is convicted of stealing
and the magistrates send him to prison for six months and
order him in addition to pay a fine of £100. If he fails to pay
the fine, an alternative of three months may be imposed to
follow the sentence of six months, thus bringing the total
imprisonment up to nine months.

Only in exceptional circumstances can young persons
between the ages of fourteen and seventeen be now sent to
prison, and children never. The powers of magistrates in
respect of juveniles are dealt with in Chapter 26.

A court of summary jurisdiction is now prohibited by the
Magistrates' Courts Act, 1952, s. 107 (2) from sending a
person under seventeen to prison.

Similar restrictions are imposed by Section 17 (2) and (3)
of the Criminal Justice Act, 1948, which provide:

'(2) No court shall impose imprisonment on a person
under twenty-one years of age unless the court is of opinion
that no other method of dealing with him is appropriate;
and for the purpose of determining whether any other
method of dealing with any such person is appropriate the
court shall obtain and consider information about the cir-

cumstances and shall take into account any information
before the court which is relevant to his character and his
physical and mental condition.

'(3) Where a court of quarter sessions imposes imprisonment on any such person as is mentioned in the last fore-
going sub-section the court shall state the reason for its
opinion that no other method of dealing with him is
appropriate.'

Delinquents of these ages will now instead be sent to
approved schools, Borstal institutions, remand and detention
centres to be set up under the new Act.

CHAPTER 21

BORSTAL

THE law relating to committals to Borstal is to be found in the Criminal Justice Act, 1948, Section 20, the second schedule to the Act, and the Magistrates' Courts Act, 1952, Section 28.

Borstal training can be ordered only for those who 'are not less than sixteen but under twenty-one' on the day they are convicted. They must be convicted of an offence for which they could have been sent to prison without the option of paying a fine.

Sentence of Borstal training may be passed at Assizes or Quarter Sessions. If the magistrates after convicting a defendant think Borstal training is desirable they have no power to pass such a sentence but must commit him to a court of quarter sessions. This court then enquires into the circumstances of the case and if it thinks it desirable may sentence the delinquent to Borstal. If not, it 'may deal with him in any manner in which the court of summary jurisdiction might have dealt with him'.

All three courts before dealing with a delinquent in this way must 'consider any report or representations made by the Prison Commissioners on the offender's physical and mental condition and his suitability for the sentence'.

To obtain this report the magistrates may remand a defendant in custody for not more than three weeks. If this is insufficient, further remands for similar periods may be made.

A delinquent sentenced to Borstal training may be detained for three years. The courts do not decide the length of his stay. This is now the responsibility of the Prison Commissioners and depends upon the progress he makes during the training.

With all these restrictions, it is easy to see that to Borstal go only the most obstinate cases of adolescent delinquency with which our penal system has to cope. Many are high-spirited young men and women who cannot for long resist the call of adventure and excitement which a raid upon organized and embattled society in the shape of crime provides. Many more, direct descendants of Autolycus, snappers-up of unconsidered trifles, have a natural bent towards petty crime, and take to thieving and allied pursuits as more happily constituted youths find escape in free verse or French verbs.

'Not one in a hundred', says a recent Report of the Borstal Association, 'can be termed a tradesman, and if in employment at all, the majority of jobs previously held have been of the "blind alley" variety. Both physically and mentally a number are found at the outset of training to be sub-average. Very many are educationally backward, and illiteracy, even in these days, is frequently met with.'

The Borstal system is often criticized because many of its inmates continue in their criminal ways after release. But when we think of the difficult material the Borstal authorities have to work upon, we should remember Doctor Johnson's talking horse: 'The wonder, Sir, is not what the animal said but that it was able to say anything at all.' If the successors to magistrates now on the bench ten or twenty years on come less frequently upon prisoners whose lists of 'previous' go back to their teens, in many cases it will be not because Borstal has had many failures but because, with the many failures, Borstal has also had many successes.

CHAPTER 22

ONE DAY

PARLIAMENT seems to have a low opinion of the entertainment value of the magistrates' courts, for one of the punishments it has devised as an alternative to imprisonment is detention within the precincts of the court for the rest of the day. This power is contained in Section 110 of the Magistrates' Courts Act, 1952.

A most useful power it is. Let us give two examples of how it is used.

A man is fined ten shillings. He has no money. The minimum alternative of imprisonment is five days. At two shillings per day, the magistrates may think that is too high. Instead therefore they order him to be detained for the day. At the rising of the court or not later than eight in the evening the man is released and that is the end of the matter.

Where magistrates have power to impose a fine but cannot inflict imprisonment without the option, they may order 'one day's detention' only as an alternative to a fine (*R*. v. *Ball* [1947], 1 All E. Reports 818).

Or the magistrates may want to record a conviction with a view to future action. A young man, for instance, has not responded satisfactorily to probation but they do not consider him ripe for Borstal. They may sentence him to 'one day'. He may think the sentence is a ludicrous one, but he would not be so happy if he knew that the adjudication will form part of his qualification for entry into Borstal if he should offend again; though a previous conviction, it should be noted, is not now essential before a sentence of Borstal detention can be imposed.

The alternative of 'one day' may also be imposed for the non-payment of a fine even where the defendant has been given time to pay. It may also be used as an alternative for the non-payment of arrears of maintenance, rates, or civil debts.

CHAPTER 23

PROBATION

DESPITE popular suspicion, there is nothing sentimental about probation. It was entirely in keeping with its undemonstrative, long-suffering character that it celebrated its legislative diamond jubilee without fuss and fury by the thorough overhaul of its provisions which we now find in Sections 3 to 12 of the Criminal Justice Act, 1948.

During these sixty years of trial and error the probation system has had to meet with a great deal of misinformed criticism from people both inside and outside the courts who feared its clemency and forbearance would increase rather than diminish crime. This is strange seeing that we ourselves in our everyday lives are continually placing our friends and acquaintances on probation. We do so for the very good reason that if we employed our more drastic punishments for every misdemeanour they would soon become so familiar as to lose all their terrors.

We tell Jane for example 'not to do this again' contenting ourselves with conviction and admonition. For more serious escapades we say that 'if this happens again, to bed you will go.' A few years pass and Jane in her turn puts us on probation. 'If you continue to behave with such Victorian narrow-mindedness,' she storms, 'I leave the house never to return,' and we fall back silent remembering the dozens of cautionary tales we have read about why girls go wrong.

All this is based on the soundest good sense. It keeps bed and abandonment at bay, threats whose terrors may flee with familiarity and investigation. Jane's quick wits may soon tell her that an afternoon in bed may be no worse than an hour spent in mastering the idiosyncrasies of English spelling and later she in her turn may realize that the housing shortage and rationing complications make the policy of the slammed door one to be reserved only for the most impossible of parents.

So it is with delinquents. Heavy-handed methods have not proved as effective in the past as is popularly supposed, and if they fail, the community may have to sit out the lifetime of a persistent crook, he on one side of a wall and we on the other, when perhaps in his earlier and more impressionable years he might have yielded to gentler methods. In any case if these gentler methods fail, there is usually plenty of time left to satisfy our itch for vengeance which is not so far below the skin as we should like to think.

The probation system allows magistrates to deal with delinquents without imposing any immediate punishment. There are three methods. The first is known as the 'Discharge Absolute'. It corresponds with our 'Don't do it again'. It is used for the hard cases that in less enlightened days made for so much bad law. It allows the letter of the law to be tempered by the spirit of equity. Generally the defendant's character is not in question. He has committed some minor offence but is able to put up some 'hard luck' story which shows him to be more sinned against than sinning – the doctor travelling at forty miles an hour on his way to the inevitable urgent case; the lady dogged by insomnia who in despair turns to intoxicants to find them only too effective when wakened on the footway by the police. Age cannot wither nor custom stale their infinite variety, and magistrates should be on their guard against dealing with too many cases in this way. No one omits to sign his motor driving licence or lets the dog out without his collar out of pure devilment. There are probably 'hard luck' stories of varying degrees of emotional intensity behind nine out of ten summonses which come up for hearing.

When charges are dealt with in this way the entry in the register should be 'Discharged absolutely'. This will distinguish the adjudication from a dismissal under the Magistrates' Courts Act, 1952, which is described in Chapter 11. The difference is important. 'Dismissed,' means that the defendant was found not guilty. 'Discharged absolutely' means that he was found guilty but the court contented itself with mak-

ing that order and did not go on to inflict punishment by
fine or imprisonment.

So much for the 'Discharge Absolute'. More serious cases
may be dealt with in two other ways. The magistrates may
discharge the delinquent 'subject to the condition that he
commits no offence' during the next twelve months or some
shorter period to be fixed by the court. Or the magistrates
may make a probation order placing the offender under the
supervision of a probation officer for anything up to three
years but not less than one year.

The great difference between the 'Discharge Absolute' and
these other two methods is that whereas with the first the
delinquent cannot afterwards be punished for that offence,
whatever his subsequent conduct may be, with the other
two types of order he does not achieve immunity so
early.

A delinquent discharged conditionally may be brought
back to the court if he commits another offence during the
period of his provisional release and punished for the original offence. The same is true if he is placed on probation,
but, in addition, as a probationer he is subject to much
greater control. 'A probation order may,' says Section 3 (3)
of the Act, 'require the offender to comply during the whole
or any part of the probation period with such requirements
as the court, having regard to the circumstances of the case,
considers necessary for securing the good conduct of the
offender or for preventing a repetition by him of the same
offence or the commission of other offences.' These conditions may range from signing the pledge to residing in a
hostel. If the probationer breaks one of them or fails to
carry one out, he may be brought back for this too and
punished for the original offence. Should the magistrates
prefer, however, he can instead be fined any sum not
exceeding ten pounds and the probation order allowed to
continue.

Until the new Act was passed every probation order took
the form of a recognizance. The probationer entered into a

bond with sureties in addition if the magistrates thought fit. If he broke the conditions of the probation order the recognizance became forfeit. A recognizance is now no longer an essential part of a probation order. In most cases it will not be thought necessary, but should the magistrates think it desirable in any particular case to require a surety, they have power to order one by Section 11 (1).

We cannot anticipate how the judges will interpret these new provisions. In the meantime, of course, the magistrates will have to decide points which may arise unaided. One question is – are the magistrates bound to proceed against a delinquent they are told has committed a further offence since his release? A careful reading of Section 8 (1) seems to indicate that they have a discretion, because the section says 'they *may* issue a summons or warrant'. 'May' in Acts of Parliament often means 'must', but we shall probably be right in this instance in thinking that it is not used imperatively, because only a few words further on we find Parliament using the word 'shall' imperatively, and we may therefore infer that the use of 'may' is deliberately intended to give the magistrates a discretion. There will probably be many cases where they will not wish to pursue the delinquent further. For the subsequent offence he may have been sent to prison or to Borstal and they may think that punishment sufficient; or again he may have been fined and they may think it preferable to allow the probation order they have already made to continue.

Apart from speculation upon the interpretation which is to be placed on the single word 'may', the whole tenor of Section 8 (1) seems to indicate that the magistrates are to consider the circumstances of each case before they decide what course to take against a backsliding probationer. Thus, they are not to issue a summons or warrant until he has been both 'convicted' *and* 'has been dealt with in respect of the (subsequent) offence' which seems to indicate that before taking any proceedings at all the magistrates are to see what course the second court has taken and then to regulate their own procedure according to what they think will be best for the delinquent.

Before the Criminal Justice Act, 1948 was passed the courts were encouraged to deal with breaches of probation orders and orders of conditional discharge informally unless it was thought desirable to make a charge so that an additional sentence of imprisonment or a fine for the original offence should be imposed.

In *R.* v. *Webb* [1953] 2 Q.B. 390, however, the judges held that merely to take breaches of probation or of a conditional discharge into consideration was wrong.

'They should be separately considered,' said Lord Goddard, 'and separate sentences should be passed so that the original offences may rank as convictions. There may be cases in which a court would think fit to make the sentences for the original and subsequent offences concurrent, but it would seem desirable that this power should only be used exceptionally; it is most important that offenders should be made to realize that discharge whether on probation or conditionally is not a mere formality and that a subsequent offence committed during the operative period of the order will involve punishment for the crime for which they were originally given the benefit of this lenient treatment.'

A conditional discharge or a probation order is usually made not because of the circumstances of the charge – often they are far from trivial – but because of the character of the delinquent. It may, for example, be his first offence or he may be young. The charge is not dismissed out of hand. During the probationary period the offender is given a chance to retrieve his lost reputation. Further, if during this period he makes good, he cannot later be punished for the offence for which he was discharged or placed on probation, though, of course, the charge will figure as an item in the criminal records and should he appear in a court after the probationary period has ended it will tell against him.

At all courts now there are at least two probation officers – one man and one woman. It is their duty 'to supervise the probationers and other persons placed under their supervision and to advise, assist, and befriend them, to inquire, in accordance with any directions of the court, into the circumstances or home surroundings of any person with a view to assisting the court in determining the most suitable method of dealing with his case, to befriend, in such cases and in such manner as may be prescribed, persons who have been released from custody and to perform such other duties as may be prescribed or may be imposed by any enactment.'

Whether a defendant is to be placed under the supervision of the probation officer is a question for the court, but it is sound practice to let the probation officer have a talk with him before the order is made. If after the interview the probation officer says that he does not think that he can be of much help, it will probably be of little use compelling him to take the case against his judgement. Usually the probation officer is only too anxious to co-operate and is prepared to undertake the supervision of a delinquent if the magistrates wish him to do so even if he thinks he can do little to reform a particular individual.

Again, the delinquent himself must consent to the probation order. If he is over fourteen, a probation order cannot be made unless he expresses willingness to comply with the requirements of the order.

The success of probation depends very largely upon the character and personality of the probation officer, but the magistrates can help him a great deal by taking a sympathetic interest in his work and problems. They should take care not to overburden him with offenders who are not in need of supervision. Defendants well endowed with friends and relatives often need none. It may be sufficient to discharge them conditionally and to let the probation officer devote his time and energy to those who are friendless and alone. Nor does it help him to go to the other extreme and load him with incorrigibles whose professions of good intentions are for court wear only.

We saw in Chapter 18 that many first offenders – nearly all youthful first offenders – are foreordained to be dealt with by some form of probation, but it will not help the probation officer to let his charges know this. The moment that they stand found guilty in the dock is the moment when they are most impressionable. A short homily from the bench on what probation means and what further misbehaviour will entail often gives the case an auspicious start. Equally helpful too are those magistrates who play Jorkins to the probation officer's Spenlow throughout the probationary period, awesome figures in the background, real and well remembered, whose presence and powers the probation officer can invoke if his charge does not respond to his efforts to reclaim him.

Whenever a defendant is dealt with by any of these three methods – the Discharge Absolute, the Discharge Conditional, or Probation – the court can award costs against him and, in addition, order him to pay such damages for injury or compensation for loss as the magistrates think reasonable up to a limit of £100.

The probation system is a remarkable growth in our penal system. It gives judges and magistrates full power to exercise the prerogative of mercy in all criminal charges, treason and murder alone excepted. It marks the lawgiver's complete if tardy recognition that it is not enough that laws be just. He must also allow those who administer them to be generous. If not, they will conspire with the rest of the community to soften their severity.

Not much more than a hundred years ago – to give one example of this phenomenon – the English criminal law required its courts to condemn to death anyone convicted of stealing property worth one shilling or more. Judges and juries combined to defeat this inhuman law, judges by discovering all sorts of technicalities invalidating the proceedings, juries by finding the value of the thing stolen to be worth eleven pence when it was obviously worth more. Penal reform abolished the death sentence for all but a few charges and gave to the courts the right to determine the sentence according to the gravity of the offence. Later followed the first tentative Probation Acts, until to-day in all cases which they are entrusted to try magistrates have unfettered discretion to temper justice with mercy.

CHAPTER 24

SURETIES TO KEEP THE PEACE

So far we have seen what can be done where an offence has been committed. But, we may ask, have the magistrates no power to check a person who is likely to commit an offence or a breach of the peace and so prevent rather than cure?

There is such a power. The magistrates may require a person they think will cause a disturbance in the future to enter into a recognizance to be of good behaviour. They may also require him to find sureties. In popular phrase they may 'bind him over to keep the peace'.

The power is a most interesting one. It probably existed before justices of the peace were called into being some six hundred years ago, and if we want to discover how it can be used and what punishment can be inflicted should the recognizance become forfeit, we must often turn not to Acts of Parliament as we have hitherto done but to cases in which the judges have considered these questions and to old text-books describing the work and powers of justices in past centuries.

Our first question then is – in what circumstances can magistrates properly require a person to enter into a recognizance to keep the peace?

First and pre-eminently they may require it where a person has been guilty of violence or has threatened violence and there are reasonable grounds for thinking he will carry out his threats.

Thus a person convicted of an assault may be ordered to enter into a recognizance instead of or in addition to any punishment inflicted for the assault.

Magistrates are most frequently asked to exercise their powers to bind over upon a summons for threats. The procedure here is defined by Section 91 of the Magistrates' Courts Act, 1952, and is intended for cases where one person has been threatened with violence by another and has good grounds for fearing that the threats may be carried out.

But the exercise of the power is not limited to where a threat is made against one particular individual. If a person himself threatens or incites others to commit acts which may imperil other persons he too may be bound over. This brings us to the case in which the well-known labour leader, George Lansbury, figured. At a time when the militant suffragette campaign was at its height, when a large number of acts of violence were being committed – the defacement of letters posted in letter boxes, the breaking of shop windows and the destruction of buildings by fire and explosives – Mr Lansbury in speeches at Westminster and Bow urged the ladies to go on with their law-breaking campaign, declaring that 'women who were outlaws ought to break the law on every possible occasion short of taking human life' (*Lansbury* v. *Riley* [1914], 3 K.B. 229, 77 J.P. 440).

Mr Lansbury was summoned to Bow Street Magistrates' Court to show cause why he should not be bound over. It was argued on his behalf that before he could be required to do that it must be shown that his behaviour had caused some particular individual to go in fear of bodily hurt.

The judges, however, held that the power could be exercised if it appeared to the magistrates that some persons might be hurt although against them personally Mr Lansbury might have had no grievance. The mischief aimed at is a breach of the peace which may be harmful to 'the King and his people' both individually and generally.

Mr Lansbury's advisers also tried to find a way of escape for him by arguing that the old Act of Edward III upon which the magistrates' power of binding over is in part founded, applied only to 'pillors and robbers' and that Mr Lansbury was neither a pillor nor a robber. In a very learned judgement, Mr Justice Avory disposed of this point saying that he believed the magistrates' power went back beyond the Act of Edward III and therefore was not restricted to the malicious characters there catalogued. Further, that in fact for generations magistrates had been binding over persons for a number of other actions. Their right to do so had not been questioned and therefore they could by 1914 claim this to be correct practice because unquestioned during long usage. To support this contention he referred to 'Dalton's Country Justice', a handbook to which magistrates turned in the days of Sir Robert Walpole.

From this work Mr Justice Avory quoted a passage which is authority for the contention that the power to bind over extends not only to what is said but equally to what is written, to publications no less than to speeches. 'Libellers,' wrote Dalton, 'also may be bound to their good behaviour, as disturbers of the peace, whether they be the contrivers, the procurers, or the publishers of the libel; for such libelling and defamation tendeth to the raising of quarrels and effusion of blood, and are especial means and occasions tending and inciting greatly to the breach of the peace.'

Sometimes the power may be used where a person proposes to do a perfectly lawful act if there are reasonable grounds for anticipating that it will end in a breach of the peace. This is illustrated by the case of *R. v. Little and Dunning*, ex parte *Wise* (1910), 74 J.P. 7. Wise was a Protestant preacher. He announced his intention to lead his Bible class through certain streets of Liverpool. Provided he caused no obstruction this was a perfectly lawful act. The streets through which he proposed to march, however, were in the Roman Catholic quarter and it was reasonably feared that the Roman Catholics would regard the afternoon's excursion as a challenge and a provocation. It was held that a breach of the peace might reasonably be feared and that the magistrates could properly require Wise to enter into a recognizance to keep the peace.

Finally the power was placed on the widest possible basis by a case differing greatly from all those we have so far considered – *R. v. Sandbach* (1935), 99 J.P. 251. The facts of the

MC–6

case illustrate a dilemma with which magistrates are sometimes faced by an incorrigible offender and the decision
shows them a very satisfactory way out.

A book-maker's look-out had been repeatedly convicted
of obstructing the police by warning his principal of their
approach. The maximum fine for this offence is £5 and presumably the betting was sufficiently lucrative to be worth
paying as many fines of £5 as the court chose to impose. The
day came, however, when the look-out was ordered not to
pay the customary fine but to enter into a recognizance of
£20 and to find two sureties in £10 each as a guarantee for
his future good behaviour.

It was argued on appeal before the judges that the magistrate had no power to make such an order because the
defendant had in no way acted violently. The judges rejected
this narrow view of the justices' powers, and Mr Justice
Humphreys in a sentence gives us a breath-taking panorama
of the catholicity of the power to bind over. 'Blackstone says
in terms that a magistrate may properly bind over a person
in any case where it is apprehended that it is likely he will
commit a breach of the peace or that he will do something
against the law.'

So much for the decisions of justices which show us in
what cases the power to bind over may be used. In others
Parliament has taken a hand by specially enacting that the
power may be used in offences for which magistrates
formerly felt doubtful that it could be properly employed
because the element of violence or the imminence of a
breach of the peace was not necessarily present. Drunkenness, for example, was one. These doubts have been dispelled
by the Licensing Act, 1902, Section 3, which allows the
magistrates to require a 'recognizance to be of good behaviour' 'in addition to or in substitution for any other
penalty' in practically all offences of which drunkenness is
the whole or part.

As we have already seen no one is bound to enter into a
recognizance. What if the defendant refuses to do so? Or

what if he cannot find the sureties? Or again what if he breaks a condition of his recognizance?

In any of these events he may be imprisoned. Mr Mead, for many years a distinguished metropolitan magistrate and a great authority not to say enthusiast upon this subject, thinks the maximum imprisonment may be for as long as twelve months. The alternative offered to Mr Lansbury was three months and in *R*. v. *Sandbach*, supra, two months. In most cases three months will probably be considered sufficient. Where proceedings are taken under the Magistrates' Courts Act, 1952, Section 91, the maximum imprisonment is six months.

R. v. *Sandbach* shows us what an effective check a 'binding over' can be. Consider the defendant's position. If he refuses to enter into the recognizance he goes to prison. If he enters into the recognizance he must either abandon his coast-guarding activities or run the risk of being arrested for a breach when not only would he be liable to imprisonment himself but his sureties must pay the sum in which they went bond. In short, the magistrate's dilemma has become the defendant's, which is very right and proper and as it should be.

A recognizance once entered into covers all forms of peace breaking. The look-out in *R*. v. *Sandbach*, supra, for example, would be liable for breach not only if later he again obstructed the police but also if he was threatening or violent.

Finally what form does procedure take? A private individual complaining of another's threats proceeds by complaint – that is a summons which is heard like other summonses. If the magistrates find that the threats have been made and there are real grounds for fearing violence from the defendant, he may be ordered to enter into a recognizance. A period of imprisonment may be fixed in default, but this is often omitted because in practice the defendant rarely refuses to be bound over.

If a person already in court, whether as party, witness, or spectator, commits an act of violence or utters a threat, no summons is necessary. The magistrates can order him to enter into a recognizance there and then.

Often after hearing the evidence in a trifling charge of assault the magistrates may come to the conclusion that both parties are to blame, a quarrelsome pair who need to be bound over not for their own benefit but for that of their long-suffering neighbours. In some cases they may decide that the person aggrieved in a charge of assault is not the informant but the defendant. In such circumstances they may let the accused go and order the accuser to enter into a recognizance. These instances show what a supple instrument the power to bind over may become.

In other cases proceedings may originate with a summons or warrant which may be laid by anyone; but in cases of public interest an information is usually laid by a police officer who has been instructed to do so. Thus upon information against Mr Lansbury, a summons was issued. The case is heard in the ordinary way and if the court finds in favour of the prosecution it orders the recognizance with an alternative period of imprisonment in default.

For a breach a summons or warrant may also be issued and again the magistrates must hear the evidence which it is thought proves that a condition has been broken. This may be followed by the evidence of the defence. In the same way proceedings may be taken against any sureties who joined in the recognizance with the prisoner.

There is no right of appeal against an order to find sureties to keep the peace (*R.* v. *London Sessions Appeal Committee*, ex parte *Beaumont* (1951), 115 J.P. 104).

CHAPTER 25

COSTS – COMPENSATION – RESTITUTION

SECTION 6 of the Costs in Criminal Cases Act, 1952, gives magistrates complete discretion to award costs to the side which wins – to the defendant if he is acquitted, to the prosecutor if the defendant is found guilty. This includes complaints for threats in pursuance of Section 91 of the Magistrates' Courts Act, 1952, to which we alluded in the last chapter, but in other cases where a recognizance to keep the peace is ordered no power to award costs exists.

Section 11 (2) of the Criminal Justice Act, 1948, allows the magistrates to award such costs as they consider proper where a defendant is placed on probation or is discharged absolutely or conditionally. In addition to this, or of course, instead, the magistrates may order the offender to pay such damages for injury or compensation for loss as they think reasonable, subject to a maximum of £100 unless the Act under which he is convicted allows a greater sum.

Counsel with more experience in the County Courts than in the magistrates' courts often ask for costs 'for the day' where a hearing is adjourned through the fault of the other side. In the County Courts this can be done, but not in the summary courts, though in the final reckoning a needless adjournment can be taken into account.

Costs granted are usually kept at a modest figure and cover little more than the expenses of the witnesses and the fees of the advocate. If awarded against an impecunious defendant they may be so low as not to cover these expenses. In their discretion the magistrates may even refuse them altogether. On the other hand, in suitable cases they may be exemplary.

Costs are rarely imposed if a defendant is sent to prison without the option of paying a fine. If a defendant is sent to prison and costs are also imposed and he fails to pay them, an additional term of imprisonment not exceeding one month may be imposed to follow the sentence for the offence.

Costs are not often granted against the prosecution if it has been undertaken by the police or a public body, such as a local authority or a government department, unless the magistrates feel that the charge ought never to have been made. The work of government could not go on unless we assume disinterestedness and impartiality in these public bodies in the execution of their responsibilities. If from time to time they charge a man who upon investigation proves to be innocent, he must be reminded should he complain of his lot of the Roman philosophy which deemed it expedient that one man should die for the State. Where, of course, it is clear that officials have not acted reasonably the court may very properly order substantial costs.

Questions of compensation are largely confined to charges of wilful damage. Section 14 of the Criminal Justice Administration Act, 1914, which is the section under which most of these charges are made, not only allows the court to impose a fine or imprisonment in punishment of the offence but allows it to order the payment of 'reasonable compensation for the damage so committed which last-mentioned amount shall be paid to the party aggrieved.'

Section 34 of the Magistrates' Courts Act, 1952 allows magistrates upon conviction for felony to award compensation 'to any person aggrieved' up to a limit of £100.

Problems of 'Restitution' usually arise upon charges of larceny, fraud, and illegal pawning. Upon conviction for theft or illegal pawning the magistrates are empowered to make an order that the stolen or improperly pawned article is to be given back to the owner. By the time the thief has been convicted the property may have been acquired by some innocent third party. The magistrates can compel him to hand it back to the lawful owner though they may compensate him for his loss by ordering in the words of the Larceny Act, 1916, Section 45 (3), that 'out of such moneys taken from the offender a sum not exceeding the amount of the proceeds of such sale be delivered to the said purchaser.'

Similarly a pawnbroker may be ordered to return an article illegally pawned where the advance is under ten pounds. In such a case, the Pawnbrokers' Act, 1872, Section 30, allows the court to make special terms by ordering the owner to repay to the pawnbroker either the whole or part of the loan 'as according to the conduct of the owner and the other circumstances of the case seem just and fitting.'

In olden days a sale in 'market overt' as, for example, at a public fair held upon regular days, gave the purchaser a good title. But to-day he enjoys no such immunity. Upon conviction the property revests in the true owner.

If it is money – notes as well as coins – which has been stolen the position is reversed, because it is essential in a civilized community to ensure that currency circulates freely. The true owner can recover his money from the thief but not from a third party who has acquired it lawfully for value, even though he is able to identify the coins or notes by marks or numbers or in any other way. He can, however, get them back from the thief if he can identify them or if the thief has passed them on to someone else for no gain to himself – if, for instance, he has made a present of it to someone or again if he had used the money to purchase goods from a person who knew the money had been stolen.

The law of Restitution is based on the conception of 'Title'. A thief may steal my book. But he cannot steal my title to it. I remain owner no matter into how many innocent hands the book passes before it is restored to me. If, however, the book is not stolen from me but I am induced to part with it voluntarily, even though by fraud or false pretences, then I have given up not only possession of the book but my title of owner. Hence if property obtained by fraud is passed on to an innocent third party, the title goes with it and no restitution order can be made in favour of the person defrauded. But an order can be made in his favour if the property is still in the hands of the defrauder.

A great deal of property falls into the hands of the police which is not the subject of a conviction for larceny but for which there are two or more claimants – for instance, property known to have been stolen but where the thief has eluded arrest or property not included in any charge for which a conviction has been obtained. A summary method of disposing of these claims is provided by the Police (Property) Act, 1897. It enables magistrates to order the delivery of any property which has come into the possession of the police to the person they consider to be the owner.

CHAPTER 26

JUVENILE COURTS

EVERYONE under seventeen who is charged with an offence or is brought before a bench of magistrates on some civil matter is a 'juvenile' and must be tried in a juvenile court unless he is charged jointly with an adult, when the proceedings take place in the ordinary court in the ordinary way.

Juvenile courts must not be held in the ordinary court room; or, if they are, they must sit on a different day or at a different time from the adult courts.

They differ in many important ways from the adult courts. Their powers to punish are much less. Their powers to order reformatory treatment are much greater.

We shall find the law relating to juvenile courts in the Children and Young Persons Act, 1933. Their objects are concisely stated in Section 44 (1) of the Act.

'Every court in dealing with a child or young person who is brought before it, either as being in need of care or protection or as an offender or otherwise, shall have regard to the welfare of the child or young person and shall in a proper case take steps for removing him from undesirable surroundings and for securing that proper provision is made for his education and training.'

Thus obscurely tucked away in the Act is a declaration of our aims in dealing with young delinquents as noble as is to be found in any criminal code past or present.

The juvenile courts are specially constituted. Not more than three justices may sit at one time. When possible at least one should be a woman. They are drawn from a panel of specially selected magistrates who in the words of a circular from the Home Secretary 'by their knowledge and sympathetic understanding of young people, or by their experience of dealing with them in various forms of social work or otherwise, appear to be most suited for the important work of the Juvenile Courts.'

The juvenile courts sit in private. But Section 47 allows to be present 'members and officers of the court, parties to the case before the court, their solicitors and counsel, and witnesses and other persons directly concerned in that case; bona fide representatives of newspapers and news agencies, and such other persons as the court may specially authorize to be present.'

In all cases, even in minor matters, the parents or guardians of a juvenile against whom proceedings are taking place should be present.

'Juveniles' are divided into two great classes which must be constantly borne in mind – 'children', persons under the age of fourteen; 'young persons', those who have attained the age of fourteen but are under seventeen.

Section 50 raises the age of criminal responsibility. No child under eight can now be found guilty of a criminal offence. Between eight and fourteen it is also presumed that the child has not reached the age of criminal responsibility, but in his case the presumption may be rebutted if there is evidence that though young in years he is old in malice. If he has committed a criminal act with reasonable competence the court may infer that he knew perfectly well that he was doing something that was wrong.

The evidence of such unhappy precocity is usually to be found in the same testimony which goes to prove that the crime has been committed. 'So,' says the robust Hale, writing in the days of Cromwell, 'an infant between the age of eight and nine years was executed for arson, it appearing that he was actuated by malice and revenge, and had perpetrated the offence with craft and cunning.' 'And,' adds another commentator, 'where an infant of nine years of age killed an infant of the like age, and confessed the felony, it appearing upon examination that he had hid both the blood and the body, the justices were of opinion that he might lawfully be hanged.'

All juveniles charged with summary offences must be dealt with in the juvenile courts. A 'young person' but not a 'child' will have the right to elect to be tried before a jury if it is an offence for which an adult may be sent to prison for more than three months except for charges of assault.

As we saw in Chapter 8 the Magistrates' Courts Act, 1952, Section 19, allows magistrates to try a large number of the less serious indictable offences if the defendant consents. The same Act in Section 21 gives them still greater powers when dealing with juveniles. A child charged with an indictable offence must be tried by them unless he is charged jointly with an adult or the charge is one of homicide. Neither the child nor his parents or guardians have the right to claim trial by jury.

Unlike a child, the consent of a young person charged with an indictable offence must (by Section 20) be obtained before the magistrates can deal with him summarily. On the other hand, the magistrates are not bound to deal summarily with a young person as they are bound to deal with a child. If the charge is one of some gravity they may commit the young person for trial as they would an adult. And, of course, a young person charged with homicide must like a child be committed and cannot be dealt with summarily.

Up to the moment when the magistrates decide whether the charge has or has not been proved, procedure in the juvenile courts in dealing with criminal charges is practically the same as in the adult courts. The general rules of procedure, of the admission of evidence and the competency of witnesses apply with equal rigour in both.

Sometimes it is obvious that a juvenile would be the better for supervision, whether at a school or under a probation officer, but, however this may be, if the juvenile disputes the charges made against him, the magistrates must take care to guard against any impatience towards rules of procedure and evidence which it may be thought stand meaninglessly in the path of a finding of guilty and ultimately the young delinquent's salvation. The net spread by the Act is wide, and if some escape its meshes when possibly it would be better for them if they were caught, it may be a matter for Parliament and amending legislation, but it cannot be an excuse for a denial of legal rights or for a failure to apply the same high standard required of the law to juveniles as to adults.

If the magistrates find that the offence with which a juvenile is charged is proved, he is no longer said to be 'convicted' or 'sentenced'. He is said to have been 'found guilty of an offence' and the method by which he is dealt is 'an order made upon such a finding'.

It may be thought that these are distinctions without differences. But the change in terms is a valuable one from two points of view. First, from the delinquent's – he may have some satisfaction later in life in feeling that he has not been stigmatized as a 'convict' or that he has served a 'sentence'. To those who have never fallen from grace these may seem small matters, but it may have a real meaning for those who in their early days have come into collision with the criminal law.

But a second and more important justification for this change is that it is a constant reminder to magistrates sitting in the juvenile courts that their efforts must ever be directed towards reclamation and never, except for delinquents who defy all attempts to save them from a career of crime, towards punishment.

The juvenile courts have been furnished with a great variety of additional methods of dealing with delinquents not found in the adult courts. All of them are directed towards reformation. Some are drastic and may determine a child's career for several years.

They may, of course, deal with a juvenile under the probation system in any way which they could deal with an adult. If charged with an offence for which an adult can be sent to prison they may commit him to the care of a 'fit person' – usually a local authority – until the age of 18, or send him to an approved school – a child for three years or until he is 15, whichever is the longer; a young person not yet 16 for three years and if 16 until he is 19.

So much for the 'reformatory powers'. Many of the 'punitive powers' have been curtailed by the Act. The power to whip disappeared with the passing of the Criminal Justice Act, 1948. A fine may be imposed but a child must not be fined more than 40s. Costs must not exceed the amount of the fine. A juvenile who does not pay the fine may be detained in a remand home. The maximum detention is a month. He may also be committed to a remand home outright if found guilty of an offence for which an adult could be sent to prison, but here again the maximum must not exceed one month. He cannot be sent to prison even if unruly or depraved.

Where, however, a young person is remanded or committed for trial, he may be sent to a remand centre if the court certifies that he is of so unruly a character that he cannot safely be detained in a remand home or of so depraved a character that he is not fit to be so detained. If no remand centre is available he may be committed to a prison. Criminal Justice Act, 1948, Section 27 (1) (b).

Parents who are often more to blame than their delinquent children may be made to suffer all or part of the consequences of the offence committed. If a child is sent to an approved school or put under the care of a fit person, the court may order his parents to contribute to his maintenance. It may also order them to pay a fine, damages, or costs. In the case of a child, the penalty must be imposed on the parent 'unless the court is satisfied that the parent or guardian cannot be found, or that he has not conduced to the offence by neglecting to exercise due care.'

In deciding which of these many ways of dealing with juvenile delinquents they should adopt, the magistrates naturally take into consideration a number of other factors besides the offence of which the defendant has been found guilty. As we saw in Chapter 18 in dealing with adults the offence was only one consideration which determined the result of the proceedings, and not necessarily the most important. Its importance is even less in dealing with juveniles. The magistrates not only may consider the reports of the police, probation officers, and local authorities. They are enjoined to do so. Upon the contents of these reports often hangs the delinquent's fate. They may make all the difference between lenient treatment under the probation system or the much more drastic order that he be sent to a school for some years.

If they are written these reports need not be read aloud for the child or his parents to hear – these may perhaps challenge the accuracy of their contents; but the court must tell them of any part of a report they consider material. This provision called forth a great deal of criticism at the time the Act became law, but in fact there is not much substance in the criticism. In the adult courts, the magistrates are constantly acting upon the contents of reports – from doctors, psychiatrists, and prison officials – without communicating the contents to the defendant about whom they are written. In the juvenile courts, reports are so voluminous, so numerous, and so decisive that their importance is much more apparent than in the adult court; but in fact the difference is only one of degree and not of principle.

The great danger of acting on a report which the defendant does not see is that if it contains inaccuracies he cannot put them right. There is less danger of such mistakes occurring in the juvenile courts than in the adult courts because there are usually at least two reports from different sources interested in the child – a probation officer and his school authorities, for instance – and the tendency should be for one to correct the other.

Besides youthful delinquents, the juvenile courts deal with another great class of children – those more sinned against than sinning, or, in the more prosaic words of Section 61 of the Act, those children or young persons 'who having no parents or guardians, or parents or guardians unfit to exercise care and guardianship or not exercising proper care and guardianship, are either falling into bad associations, or exposed to moral danger, or beyond control'.

Cases brought under this section range from children

abandoned or ill-treated by their parents to young girls running wild in the streets on the eve of entering upon a life of prostitution.

If the magistrates do come to the conclusion that a juvenile so brought before them is in need of care or protection, they may commit him to an approved school, place him under the care of a fit person, call upon his parents to enter into a recognizance to exercise proper care and guardianship, or put him under the supervision of a probation officer.

Juveniles under this section are brought before the court by persons unconnected with their families – often a constable, or a probation officer. The parent either contests the charges of neglect or does not bother to resist them. But in some cases a juvenile may be running amok and the distressed parent can do nothing to control him. In such a case the parent himself may bring the juvenile into court and call upon the magistrates for their help. This is permitted by Section 64, and if the magistrates are satisfied that the child is in fact beyond the control of the parent, they may send him to an approved school or place him under supervision. Section 65 gives similar powers to a poor law authority which has a refractory child in one of its institutions.

Such in brief outline is the juvenile court of to-day. We cannot compare it with the juvenile courts of a hundred years ago because a hundred years ago juvenile courts and adult courts were one. But our literature contains a very vivid picture of the trial of a juvenile at that time. In Chapter Eleven of *Oliver Twist* is an account of the proceedings which took place before Mr Fang when Oliver was falsely accused of stealing an old gentleman's pocket handkerchief. After a trial which can be described only as a travesty of justice, Oliver was sentenced out of hand to three months' imprisonment. Only the timely intervention of the bookseller at whose stall the old gentleman was standing saved him from serving the sentence.

The Oliver Twists of our time run no risk of such treatment. In points of detail the juvenile courts as we know them may be fairly criticized, but viewed broadly there are few of our legal institutions about which we can be so confident that we have made changes for the better. The juvenile delinquent does not now step into a dock from which an old lag has just stepped down. The old lag is not the only person to speak a friendly word to him after his appearance before the magistrates. We do not disgrace ourselves whilst disgracing him by sending him to prison and there arraying him in convict's garb complete to the last broad arrow. In ending all this, in replacing it with better things, we have achieved something of which we may be justly proud.

CHAPTER 27

INDICTABLE OFFENCES

In Chapter 8 we defined an indictable offence as 'a crime which when the person charged with committing it is first brought before the magistrates cannot be dealt with by them but must be committed for trial at assizes or quarter sessions.'

In the same chapter we also saw that indictable offences may be divided into two great classes – those which the Magistrates' Courts Act, 1952, empowers the magistrates to deal with summarily and those which must be committed for trial at assizes or quarter sessions. It is with this latter class that we are now dealing.

A person accused of an indictable offence may be committed for trial for one of four reasons: because he is accused of an offence which the magistrates are not authorized to try in any event – as, for example, murder, manslaughter, burglary, and similar grave offences; secondly, because, although the offence may be one which the magistrates are authorized to try, they think the proper course is to commit the accused because of the exceptional circumstances of the case – a man charged with stealing £10,000, for instance; thirdly, because the prosecution is being carried on by the Director of Public Prosecutions or a public body and they do not consent to the charge being dealt with summarily; finally, because, although the offence could be tried summarily, the defendant does not consent to this course.

The magistrates in dealing with an indictable offence which the prosecution is asking them to commit for trial are not trying the case. The proceedings are accurately termed a 'preliminary examination', outwardly very much like a trial, inwardly very different.

If then they are not a trial what is their purpose? There are two. The first is to see if, after all the witnesses have been called, there is sufficient evidence to justify the expense and anxiety of putting the accused person upon his trial. Here we find another phase of the great criminal clearing house which the magistrates' courts in practice are. But for this 'preliminary examination', an accused person might be arrested and kept in prison until the next assizes – possibly three months ahead – when it might be found that there was no case against him justifying his detention. Moreover, even if the magistrates do decide there is a case for him to answer, he has the advantage of appealing to them – an independent tribunal – to allow him to be released on bail until the day of his trial.

This first purpose of the preliminary examination is to safeguard the defendant. The second purpose is to ensure that the evidence of the witnesses is recorded immediately, so that if anything happens to them before the trial, which may not take place for some months, their depositions can be read at the trial. The evidence of the witnesses is written down by the clerk, read over to them, and signed by them in acknowledgement of their accuracy. These records are known as the 'depositions'. If by the time the trial takes place a witness has died or is too ill to travel or has been spirited away by the other side, his deposition may be read instead at the court of trial on proof that it was correctly taken during the preliminary examination before the magistrates.

From the fact that the proceedings before the magistrates are an investigation and not a trial, a number of consequences flow.

The first in importance is that the proceedings need not be held in public nor need they be held in any room regularly used as a court. They are as valid if they take place in a private sitting room as in the usual court house. In emergencies as we shall see in Chapter 29 this is a most useful point to remember. In the ordinary practice of the court, it is usually convenient to go through the list of charges in the same court room, taking summary charges and indictable offences as they come and allowing the public who come in as a right to be present at summary trials to remain as a privilege at the preliminary examinations. But when occasions arise as they do when it is convenient to take a deposition elsewhere, the magistrates are perfectly entitled to do so.

A second consequence of the proceedings being an investigation and not a trial is that if the magistrates consider that the prosecution has not produced sufficient evidence to justify putting the accused upon his trial, he is discharged but he is not acquitted. This 'discharge' is not a final decision because the accused has not been tried. If later the prosecution can bring further evidence they may start proceedings afresh when again the magistrates must decide whether to discharge or commit for trial. Once the accused has been committed and acquitted by a jury he can never again be charged with the same offence, no matter what evidence may later be found to prove that in fact he did commit the crime. The acquittal is the end of the matter.

A case is recorded of a butcher who after acquittal at assizes of murder openly went about boasting that he had committed the crime. If he had been so indiscreet as to do so when he had been merely discharged by the magistrates after a preliminary examination, he could have been recharged, his admissions could have been tendered as additional evidence against him and would doubtless have been sufficient to secure his committal and very likely his conviction.

CHAPTER 28

PRELIMINARY EXAMINATION OF INDICTABLE OFFENCES

PROCEDURE during the preliminary examination of indictable offences is very similar to that followed in the trial of summary offences.

In this chapter we shall see in what respects the proceedings differ. The law which regulates them is contained in Sections 4 to 12 of the Magistrates' Courts Act, 1952.

As we saw in Chapter 9 the venue or jurisdiction for summary offences is the district in which the offence is committed. The venue for indictable offences is wider. Not only may justices deal with indictable offences committed within their jurisdiction. They may also deal with a person apprehended within it though the offence with which he is charged was committed without. In practice they rarely do so. It is usually much more convenient to take the proceedings where the offence is alleged to have been committed, because most of the witnesses reside in that district and often the local police have already taken the matter up.

In dealing with indictable offences, we frequently meet the criminal careerist – the professional who commits offences in a number of districts. He may be dealt with for all these offences by the magistrates of any jurisdiction in which he has committed one of the offences or in which he may be found. A burglar, for example, who is alleged to have committed an offence in a dozen towns may be charged before the magistrates of any one of them. Persons charged together with committing the same offence or two associated offences such as stealing and receiving may also be proceeded against before the same bench. A suitcase, for instance, may be stolen in Lancaster and received in York. Charges against both thief and receiver may be dealt with either in Lancaster or York.

To avoid disputes about boundaries, the Magistrates'

Courts Act, 1952, Section 3, provides that the jurisdiction of any court extends five hundred yards beyond its frontiers. This legal 'two men's land' one thousand yards wide running along the boundaries of all rival jurisdictions effectively avoids profitless argument over niceties of demarcation. By the same Act, an offence which is committed in a conveyance during a journey can be dealt with in any jurisdiction through which the vehicle passed.

As in the trial of summary offences, proceedings in the preliminary examination of indictable offences may begin by summons or warrant issued by a magistrate; or the defendant may be arrested by a constable without either.

Applications to magistrates are rarely made for a summons or warrant if the charge is a felony. The police may do so if the defendant disappears and they think he may re-emerge in a district where he is unknown and a warrant will more readily achieve his arrest; or if he has gone to Scotland, Ireland, or the Channel Islands, as the authorities there usually refuse to make an arrest unless they are assured a magistrate's warrant is in existence.

A private prosecutor may apply for a warrant where the police have refused to act because they think the allegations made insufficient to justify an arrest.

Warrants granted for indictable offences must be upon sworn written information. If a summons is granted the information need not be made upon oath nor need it be in writing. It is served in the same way as a summons for a summary offence.

Proceedings for summary offences as a general rule must be begun within six months of the day when they are committed. There is no such limitation for indictable offences. These charges may be made years after the offence was committed. Eugene Aram is chiefly remembered to-day because he was hanged for a murder he had committed fourteen years before. To this general rule there are a few unimportant exceptions – the Blasphemy Act, 1697, four days; the Riot Act, 1714, Section 8, twelve months; the

Criminal Law Amendment Act, 1885, Section 5, twelve months, are examples.

Witnesses both for the prosecution and the defence may be compelled to give evidence and produce documents as in summary cases. Witnesses who refuse to attend or to give evidence may be imprisoned for seven days or 'until they sooner give evidence.'

In Chapter 12 we saw that certain persons could not be called as witnesses in the trial of a summary offence. In legal phrase, they are incompetent. They are equally incompetent in the preliminary examination of an indictable offence. In the following chapter we saw that even competent witnesses could not tell the court everything they might know about the defendant or the charge, some evidence being inadmissible. Similar evidence would be equally inadmissible during a preliminary examination. Generally speaking the rules of evidence are the same whether the magistrates are trying a summary offence or are taking the evidence in an indictable charge.

During the trial of summary offences, defendants need not be present. A very large number are dealt with in their absence, though in practice where the magistrates have the power to send a defendant to prison without the option of a fine they invariably insist upon his attendance. Defendants accused of indictable offences must always be present and no proceedings will be valid in their absence. To this rule the only exception is the prisoner who behaves so obstreperously whilst before the magistrates that the hearing cannot go on.

Only one justice need sit during the hearing of a preliminary examination, though in practice there are usually two and often more. Where the examination occupies a number of hearings only those justices who have sat throughout can decide whether the defendant is to be committed or discharged; and, of course, there must be at least one justice who has been present all through the examination. If there is only one, he alone can decide between committal and discharge.

The depositions are taken down by the clerk. He does it on behalf of his magistrates. It is for them to decide what shall go in and what shall be left out if any question arises of the admissibility of what is tendered as a piece of evidence, though they will generally be guided in this by the clerk.

As for summary offences, the witnesses are sworn, they give their evidence in chief, are cross-examined and re-examined. Everything they say which is relevant and admissible should be included in the deposition. At the end, the clerk reads it over to the witness, thus giving him an opportunity of correcting any mistakes. When he is satisfied as to the correctness of the deposition he must sign it.

Sometimes at the second or subsequent proceedings it is impossible to obtain the attendance of any one magistrate who sat during the preceding hearing and an entirely new bench has to be summoned. The witnesses in such an event must be recalled and resworn, but it will not be necessary to rewrite their depositions as they have already been taken in the presence of the defendant.

If, however, half-way through the proceedings another defendant is arrested and charged with the first, not only must the witnesses be recalled but they must be re-examined in the presence of the new defendant and the depositions must be written out again, because the newcomer is entitled not merely to hear the deposition read aloud but to see the witnesses under examination, to object if he wishes to the admission of evidence and to protest if the witness is led.

When all the witnesses for the prosecution have given their evidence, the magistrates must consider whether the case is sufficiently strong to justify committing the defendant for trial. Section 7 of the Magistrates' Courts Act, 1952, puts it in this way. 'If a magistrates' court inquiring into an offence as examining justices is of opinion, on consideration of the evidence and of any statement of the accused, that there sufficient evidence to put the accused upon trial by jury for any indictable offence, the court shall commit him for trial; and if it is not of that opinion, it shall, if he is in custody for no other cause than the offence under enquiry, discharge him.'

As we saw in Chapter 16 in the trial of summary offences before convicting a defendant, the magistrates must be satisfied that the charge is proved beyond reasonable doubt. No such high degree of proof is required for a committal to Assizes or Quarter Sessions. Speaking of another Act drawn up in similar terms, Mr Justice Swift explained it in these words. 'The section means that there must be such evidence that if it be uncontradicted at the trial a reasonable-minded jury may convict upon it.'

The justices must not ask themselves the question which the jury will have to answer – 'Did this defendant commit this offence?' Nor must they envisage a special jury which might be empanelled, but a jury of average men and women charitable in judgement but alive to their civic responsibility. They must not, for example, ask – 'Could twelve men be found who would convict?' Twelve men can be found if we look far enough who will convict anybody of anything. Perhaps the best way of putting the question is 'Might twelve men selected at random and guided by a Judge of the High Court unanimously think the defendant guilty on the evidence as we have heard it?'

If the magistrates decide to discharge the accused, that will be the end of proceedings against him, at least until the unlikely event of the prosecution discovering further evidence and charging him afresh. The defendant leaves the court and the chairman marks the register 'Discharged, Magistrates' Courts Act, Section 7' to distinguish this decision from 'Dismissed, Magistrates' Courts Act, s. 13'. It is most important that these entries should be made unambiguously, because as we have already seen the first is not a final acquittal, whereas the second is, and no further proceedings can be brought after it has been made.

If, on the other hand, the magistrates think the evidence is sufficiently strong to justify a committal, they then proceed with the examination as directed by Rule 5 of the

Magistrates' Courts Rules, 1952. The charge is explained to the defendant in language that he can understand. He is then told, 'You will have an opportunity to give evidence on oath before us and to call witnesses. But first I am going to ask you whether you wish to say anything in answer to the charge. You need not say anything unless you wish to do so; and you have nothing to hope from any promise, and nothing to fear from any threat that may have been held out to you to make any admission or confession of guilt. Anything you say will be taken down and may be given in evidence at your trial. Do you wish to say anything in answer to the charge?'

The defendant is then asked if he wishes to make a statement. He can do so unsworn from the dock if he chooses. Whatever he may say is written down by the clerk and if the defendant wishes to sign this statement he may. It will be sent to the court of trial with the depositions.

Next the defendant must be asked if he wishes to give evidence and afterwards call witnesses on his behalf. If he does he will give his evidence upon oath from the witness box like other witnesses. Like them too he will be subjected to cross-examination and will be liable to prosecution under the Perjury Acts if he deliberately or recklessly gives false evidence. What he and his witnesses say is taken down in the form of depositions and sent with the depositions of the witnesses for the prosecution to the court of trial.

Nothing must be done to discourage the defendant from setting out his defence at the preliminary examination. As we saw in Chapter 14, the sooner a defence is advanced the greater is the respect it may claim. Sometimes magistrates are impatient when the defendant announces his intention to set up his defence before he is committed. If the evidence for the prosecution is very strong they may feel that it can make no difference to the decision to commit. This is, of course, wrong. The ultimate decision to commit should not be made until the defendant and his witnesses have been heard. To decide in advance that the case for the prosecution cannot be overthrown is to prejudge it. Further, even if the defendant is committed, he will be able to say: 'I set out my defence before an independent tribunal at the earliest opportunity I had. For that reason I ask you to give it greater weight.' 'If the defence,' said Mr Justice Wills, 'is an honest one it should be given at the earliest possible stage, and justices should impress that upon all prisoners: otherwise the value of the defence is much lessened.'

After hearing the defendant and his witnesses, if any, the magistrates must again review the evidence and decide whether taking into account this new evidence they will still be justified in committing the defendant or whether they shall now discharge him. Unless the defendant has been particularly unfortunate in his efforts, he will have shown the existence of a conflict of evidence; but a conflict the result of which should be left to the determination of a jury unless the magistrates now feel that no jury will be likely to convict in such a case.

The magistrates are not bound to commit a defendant for trial upon the charges for which he has been brought before them. They can commit him for any charge which they consider has been disclosed in the depositions and may refuse to commit him upon a charge which the prosecution has made but which the magistrates think has not been made out. This is another consequence of the fact that during a preliminary examination the defendant is not upon his trial and cannot complain during the proceedings before the magistrates that he has not had fair warning of the exact charges he will have to meet when he is tried.

The most serious indictable offences cannot be tried at Quarter Sessions. They must be sent to the Assizes. These crimes range from treason and murder to most forms of forgery, perjury, and counterfeiting coin.

But offences which can be tried at Quarter Sessions should not be sent to the Assizes unless they are unusually grave or complex.

By the Magistrates' Courts Act, 1952, Section 10 (1),

month must pass before the next Assizes or Quarter Sessions is held to which the defendant would ordinarily be committed, he may be sent instead to any other Assize or Quarter Sessions which will be held earlier.

Witnesses both for the prosecution and the defence are bound over in a recognizance to appear at the court of trial to give their evidence. If they fail to attend the recognizance becomes forfeit. Where the defendant announces, during the preliminary examination, his intention to plead guilty, the magistrates may bind over the witnesses conditionally, which means that they will not be required to attend at the trial unless they get further notice. Witnesses giving evidence of a formal character or which is not contested – a bank clerk, for instance, producing a copy of an account – may also be bound over conditionally.

During the preliminary examination, the magistrates may remand the hearing from time to time. If on bail the defendant may be remanded for any reasonable period; but if not, the remand must not exceed 'eight clear days', that is to say, he must be brought up again not later than the ninth day.

Very similar considerations determine the grant of bail during a preliminary examination as during a summary trial. In fairness to the defendant he should be released whenever possible.

Magistrates have no right to grant bail to a person charged with treason. In felonies and misdemeanours they may refuse bail or grant it in their discretion. If they refuse bail to a person when committing him for trial for a misdemeanour, they must inform him of his right to apply for bail to a judge of the High Court.

CHAPTER 29

EMERGENCY DEPOSITIONS

MANY justices go through the whole of their magisterial career without having to take a deposition in an emergency. But one can never count upon immunity, and if the call comes it is as well to have a clear notion beforehand of what we are about, because it will be made only in the most grave cases – usually murder, manslaughter, abortion, and the like. The deposition taken may be vital to conviction. The defendant will attack it upon any technical point however small if he thinks that by doing so he can shut it out at the trial.

First then let us see in which charges an emergency deposition can be taken. Until recent years it could be taken only during the preliminary examination of indictable offences. The Magistrates' Courts Act contains no provisions for the admission of the evidence of an absent witness which correspond to the provisions by which a deposition can be admitted at a trial at Assizes or Quarter Sessions. Hence as a general rule an emergency deposition cannot be put in at the trial of a summary offence or of an indictable offence dealt with summarily, though as we shall see this difficulty can sometimes be surmounted in practice.

The exceptions to this rule arise at the rarest intervals under the Children and Young Persons Act, 1933, Sections 42 and 43, which allow the deposition of a juvenile unable to attend court through illness or injury to be read at the summary trial of a person charged with an offence of cruelty or misconduct to him.

Secondly an emergency deposition must not be confused with a 'dying declaration'. As we saw in Chapter 15 a 'dying declaration' is admissible only in charges of homicide; the declarant is not sworn, his desperate plight being considered as sufficient guarantee that he will not bear false witness upon the threshold of eternity. Further, any competent and credible person can give evidence of the declaration. He need not be a magistrate. An emergency deposition on the other hand may be taken for any indictable offence, but it must be taken by a justice and the witness must be sworn.

Some writers on this subject talk about a 'dying deposition'. No such monstrosity is known to our law. The term seems appropriate only to the deposition of a witness who fails to come up to his proof at the trial.

Now let us come to the emergencies which may happen. Most of these will present no difficulties if it is borne in mind, first, that in taking the depositions of witnesses in preliminary examinations one magistrate constitutes a court, and, secondly, that he need not sit in open court but may sit in any place convenient to himself in the discharge of his duties. Thus is happens occasionally that a witness is too ill to attend court. In such an event the court can attend the witness. The defendant, of course, must be present and must have as full an opportunity of cross-examining the witnesses as in the usual court room. The examining magistrate or magistrates must be present throughout the hearing when all the witnesses including the sick witness give their evidence. If the emergency occurs when the hearing is part way through and it is not possible to secure the attendance of any magistrate who has taken part in the examination up to this moment, those witnesses who have already given evidence before other magistrates will have to be recalled and their evidence read over to them in the presence of the magistrate who has taken the deposition of the sick witness.

If the witness is able to sign his deposition he should do so. Failing this he may make his mark, usually a cross. But the deposition will be admissible if he is incapable even of this if he understood it when it was read to him and he assented to it.

The deposition is sent to the court of trial with the other depositions and if the sick witness is unable to attend his deposition can be read to the jury as can that of any other witness unable to attend for similar reasons.

What if the evidence of a witness who is unable to attend through illness is needed in a charge which the parties wish to be dealt with summarily but which the defendant is contesting? The difficulty can be met by treating the proceedings as a preliminary examination until the evidence of the sick person has been taken. After this the defendant can be asked if he wishes to be dealt with summarily. If he so consents, the charge can then proceed summarily and the magistrates in arriving at their decision will be entitled to take into consideration the evidence of the sick person.

Cases sometimes occur where the magistrates with the consent of the defendant have decided to deal summarily with an indictable offence when it is discovered that a witness cannot attend through illness. Formerly the magistrates were entitled to reverse their decision to try the offence summarily and in such a case they could take this course to enable them to hear the witness at his bedside. This however is not now permissible since the Magistrates' Courts Act, 1952, Section 24, provides that 'a magistrates' court having begun to try an information for any indictable offence summarily shall not thereafter proceed to inquire into the information as examining justices'.

Thus where a defendant has been charged, the emergency of a witness unable to attend court need give no anxiety. The golden rule is: Whenever possible deal with the charge just as the magistrates would any other charge of which they were conducting the preliminary examination in accordance with the Magistrates' Courts Act, 1952. To point the moral let us see what happened where a magistrate did not follow this rule but for reasons best known to himself took a deposition under the Criminal Law Amendment Act, 1867, Section 6, which has now been largely replaced by Section 41 of the Magistrates' Courts Act. The defendant was charged with rape. The prosecutrix was the witness, who was unable to travel. The defendant was brought into the girl's room and her deposition was taken in his presence and that of the committing magistrate. If he had purported to commit the defendant under the old Indictable Offences Act no exception could have been taken to the proceedings. But the later Act requires that 'notice in writing of the intention to take such a statement shall be served upon the person against whom it is proposed to tender it.' This written notice was not given. The magistrate no doubt regarded it as a work of supererogation as the defendant was in custody and had no choice but go when he was bid. The failure to observe this technicality, however, destroyed not only the deposition of the prosecutrix but with it the whole case, for because of its omission the conviction was quashed. *Via trita, via tuta.* Along the oft-travelled road we shall not take the wrong turn.

But occasions arise when the magistrates can do nothing under the provisions generally employed for the hearing of a preliminary examination and when recourse must reluctantly be had to Section 41. Reluctantly because the Section is difficult. Powers it gives with one hand it takes almost completely away with the other – almost, but not quite. Rare as these occasions are, an emergency may arise when a deposition taken under it may obtain a conviction and when a failure to do so would mean the escape of the wrongdoer. It is well to have some foreknowledge of the provision. If ever an emergency does occur, someone is sure to bring it to notice, and in the excitement magistrates may be forgiven for thinking upon the first hurried perusal that it gives them much greater powers than in fact it does.

Here is the section in full:

'Where a person appears to a justice of the peace to be able and willing to give material information relating to an indictable offence or to any person accused of an indictable offence, and –

'(a) the justice is satisfied on a representation made by a duly qualified medical practitioner that the person able and willing to make the statement is dangerously ill and unlikely to recover; and

'(b) it is not practicable for examining justices to take the evidence of the sick person in accordance with the provisions of this Act and the Rules,

'the justice may take in writing the deposition of the sick person on oath.

'(2) A deposition taken under this section may be given in evidence before examining justices enquiring into an information against the offender or in respect of the offence to which the deposition relates, but subject to the same conditions as apply, under Section 6 of the Criminal Law Amendment Act, 1867, to its being given in evidence upon the trial of the offender or offence.'

The conditions imposed by the Criminal Law Amendment Act are:

(a) That the person who made the statement is dead, or that there is no reasonable possibility that he will be able to travel or give evidence.

(b) That it is proved to the court that notice, in writing, of the intention to take the statement was served upon the person (whether prosecutor or accused) against whom it is proposed that the statement should be read.

(c) That the statement is signed by the justice.

(d) That the prosecutor or the accused had or might have had, had he chosen to be present, full opportunity of cross-examining the person who made the statement.

The last condition overrides the whole of what precedes it. Hence any deposition taken under it will have no practical value unless some person has already been charged with an offence or is likely to be charged with an offence. This must be so because the deposition cannot be admitted at a subsequent trial unless the person against whom it is submitted had written notice that the deposition was to be taken and had reasonable opportunity of being present.

It is most important that the directions set out in the section in such careful detail should be complied with to the letter. For instance, if the magistrates omit to state in the caption or heading to the deposition where it was taken, it may be held to be inadmissible.

Two practical examples will illustrate the rare occasions when Section XI can be of use and when nothing can be done under any other provision.

A girl is dying, victim of a clumsy abortionist. She cannot make a dying declaration because she is full of hope of recovery. The doctors tell the police that she may survive one interview but that two will be too much for her. If they take a statement from her to support an application for a warrant, she will be unlikely to be able to make a deposition before a magistrate. The police know who the abortionist is and in proceeding under Section 41 of the Magistrates' Courts Act, 1952 and Section 6 of the Criminal Law Amendment Act they can reduce two proceedings to one. Under it, a magistrate can proceed to take a deposition if he is satisfied that a crime has been committed and he can invite the prospective defendant to be present. If he later becomes the defendant in fact, the deposition will be admissible against him. Thus in the instance we have considered, the magistrate would give written notice to the abortionist of his intention to take the deposition. If later the girl dies, and the abortionist is actually charged, the deposition can be tendered with good hope of being admitted and may very well form the most vital piece of evidence.

Again, to take a second example. A preliminary examination is taking place in Kent of an offence which has been committed in that county. A witness is taken ill in Oxford. None of the Kent examining justices is available to go to him. Nothing can be done under the general provisions of the Magistrates' Courts Act because under it the Oxford justices have no jurisdiction. But under Section 41, an Oxford magistrate may take the deposition of the witness and forward it to the court of trial where it will be added to the other depositions taken in Kent. Here again written notice will have to be given to the defendant and if he is on bail a reasonable opportunity of getting to Oxford. If in custody he can be taken there at a pace more consonant with the exigencies of the prosecution than with his own inclination.

MC–7

These instances illustrate the two chief differences between taking a deposition under the normal procedure laid down in Rule 5 of the Magistrates' Courts Rules and under the abnormal procedure provided by Section 41 of the Magistrates' Courts Act, 1952 and Section 6 of the Criminal Law Amendment Act, 1867. First under the latter an effective deposition can be taken before proceedings have been launched. Secondly, a magistrate is not limited in jurisdiction as he is under Section 2 of the Magistrates' Courts Act, 1952. Any justice can inquire into any indictable offence no matter where committed. But for Section 41, magistrates broadly speaking may act only where the offence is committed within their own district or where the defendant is found within it.

As both these examples show, charges in which the later Act can be used are few indeed, but they also show that they do occur. Upon the readiness of a magistrate to seize the opportunities that do arise may depend the success of an important prosecution.

Finally we must note that whenever a magistrate is called upon to take a deposition in an emergency it is his duty to do so, though it may possibly be at great personal inconvenience. Commenting upon the inaction of a magistrate who had refused to leave his court to take the evidence of a sick witness, Mr Justice Darling said, 'If it is practicable for him to go he must go. The question whether it is practicable or not is for the magistrate to decide in the exercise of his judicial discretion' (*R.* v. *Bros* ex parte *Hardy* [1911], 1 K.B. 159).

CHAPTER 30

APPEALS

SOME magistrates resent appeals. They look upon them not only as a challenge to their wisdom but as calling into question their good faith. They will do nothing to help the appellant against their decision.

Some welcome appeals. They greet the announcement of an intention to appeal with enthusiasm and enquire earnestly how best, short of becoming the appellant's surety, they can facilitate the enterprise; so much so that the appellant smells that most potent of all smells, the rat which is not there. He remembers with Hamlet that a man may smile and smile and be a villain. He abandons his appeal, since we would most of us 'rather bear those ills we have Than fly to others that we know not of'.

The best and surely the proper course is to preserve a judicial impassivity, to imitate the demeanour of Aristides who was so good and just that the Athenians held a plebiscite as to whether he should be expelled from the city. During the election an illiterate peasant approached Aristides and asked him to record his vote. 'Do you want to vote for expulsion?' asked Aristides, taking the man's oyster shell on which the vote was to be recorded. 'Yes,' replied the peasant, and Aristides duly recorded the vote.

Appeals from the decisions of justices made during the hearing of criminal charges are of two kinds – appeals to the justices at Quarter Sessions and appeals to judges of the Queen's Bench Division – usually known as 'appeals by case stated'.

It may be some consolation to new magistrates who are apprehensive of appeals and who think the smallest slip will be pounced upon for post mortem at a higher court to know that the likelihood of an appeal against any particular decision to Quarter Sessions is very small – according to the criminal statistics about one in seven hundred and fifty cases; whilst the probability of an appeal to the judges 'by case stated' is far more remote still.

Appeals to Quarter Sessions are by far the more numerous. In the counties they are made to the county justices at Quarter Sessions; in the boroughs to the Recorder. In the strict sense of the word they are not appeals at all. By an 'appeal' we usually mean the removal of a cause from an inferior to a superior court for the purpose of testing the soundness of the decision of the inferior court. Quarter Sessions does not examine into what has been done by the summary court. The case is completely re-heard. The prosecutor is again called upon to prove the charge. Neither side is bound by what it did or said at the first hearing. Additional witnesses may be called. In short, the proceedings are not so much an appeal as a right given to the defendant to try his luck a second time at a more leisured tribunal.

Appeals to the judges of the Queen's Bench Division, on the other hand, are appeals in the true sense of the word. Unless there is no evidence to justify their findings, the judges accept the facts of the case as the magistrates found them and limit their enquiry to questions of law. The question of law they may be asked to decide may arise not only in summary proceedings but also during the trial of an indictable offence dealt with summarily. An appeal cannot be made upon a point of law arising during the preliminary examination of an indictable offence; but an irregularity in the proceedings may be considered by the judge at Assizes or later by the Court of Criminal Appeal and if sufficiently grave may invalidate the committal. It may not be the point on which the charge was decided but a subsidiary point, a question of evidence, the competency of a witness, for instance, or a question of procedure.

The appeal to Quarter Sessions cannot be made upon any particular decision taken during the hearing of the charge but only against the decision as a whole. Moreover whereas the defendant can appeal against his conviction or sentence, the prosecutor cannot appeal to Quarter Sessions against an acquittal. But if he thinks the magistrates have made a mistake in law, he can appeal upon this question to the Divisional Court.

Let us illustrate these points with the case of *Bryant* v. *Marx* outlined in Chapter 3.

In the summary court the police, who were the prosecutors, lost the case. Their only remedy by way of appeal was to take the step they did – to appeal against the decision to the judges of the Divisional Court on the ground that the magistrate had made a mistake in law. They could not appeal to Quarter Sessions. Only the defendant could have done that if he had been convicted. The police did appeal to the Divisional Court, with the result that the magistrate's decision was reversed.

Suppose instead of acquitting the motorist the magistrate had convicted him. To him would have then been open either of the two methods of appeal – either but not both. He could have appealed to Quarter Sessions for a re-hearing both on the facts and the law or he could have appealed to the Divisional Court on the question of law alone.

Bryant v. *Marx* is a good example of what the lawyer means by a question of fact and a question of law. It was a question of fact whether the car had been left on the footway. On this both police and defendant were agreed that it had. Then came the question of law – did 'road' include 'footway' and so bring the car owner within the law of obstruction?

Bryant v. *Marx* is also a good example of how, by means of appeal by case stated, the prosecution can upset a decision on the plea that the magistrates have misinterpreted a word or phrase in an Act or regulation. But by means of an appeal of this kind, the prosecution can also upset a decision by attacking it not piecemeal but fundamentally.

An example of this is the case of *Bracegirdle* v. *Oxley* [1947], 1 All E.R. 126. Here the police summoned the driver of a heavy lorry for driving at a speed which was dangerous to the public. The maximum speed permitted for a lorry of the type was twenty miles per hour. The defendant was driv-

ing at speeds varying between forty and forty-four miles per
hour. He passed another lorry without making any sign and
crossed a narrow bridge without slackening speed.

The police asked the magistrates to say that all these facts
added up to the offence of dangerous driving. The magistrates thought they fell short of what was needed, whereupon
the police asked the judges to say whose arithmetic they
thought was right. The court, composed of the unusually
large number of five judges, had no hesitation in deciding
that the police were right and the case was sent back to the
magistrates to convict, Lord Goddard, the Lord Chief
Justice, commenting severely, 'It was impossible to say that
any reasonable-minded bench would have arrived at the
decision of the justices in the present case.'

'The Court,' he explained in the course of his judgement,
'did not sit as a general court of appeal from justices, as did
courts of Quarter Sessions. It only sat to review justices'
decisions on points of law, being bound by the facts which
they found, provided always that there was evidence on
which the justices could reach their conclusion. Perverse
decisions of justices were in the same situation as decisions
reached without evidence to support them.'

Nor should the magistrates regard their power to discharge without penalty as a heaven-sent sanctuary designed
to save them, as much as the defendant, from difficult
decisions. Many a bench has incurred the displeasure of the
judges in dealing with a case in this way when they should
have exercised their powers more drastically.

An example of this is the case of *White* v. *Hurrell's Stores
Ltd* (1941), 105 J.P. 105, where the defendant company was
summoned for selling bacon without requiring the surrender
of the appropriate coupons. The justices thought the offence
of a trivial nature and dismissed the proceedings.

'To my mind,' commented Mr Justice Humphreys, 'it is
most disturbing to find that a bench of magistrates can be
found to take the view that the offence was so trivial that
they went out of their way, in spite of a plea of guilty, to

dismiss the information under the Probation of Offenders Act. There was not the smallest pretence that the company had been tricked or deceived into committing the offence. The justices appear to have overlooked the fact that the rationing of food is an essential part of the successful carrying on of the war in which the country is engaged. To find a bench of magistrates treating a deliberate breach of such a regulation as trivial at such a time is most disturbing.'

A successful appeal at Quarter Sessions decides nothing except the charge itself. The decision is not binding on the court from which the appeal came or on any other court. A decision upon a point of law by a Divisional Court, however, is binding on all inferior courts until reversed by a higher court. Thus if Quarter Sessions decides that 'footway' includes 'road' it will not prevent justices sitting in a summary court from holding at a later date that 'footway' does not include 'road'. But when the judges in the Divisional Court decided that 'footway' included 'road' – as indeed they did – then 'footway' includes 'road' for all subsequent cases both at Quarter Sessions and in the summary courts.

An appeal to Quarter Sessions against conviction can be made only if the defendant pleaded 'not guilty'. Hence the importance of carefully recording all pleas in the court register. A defendant who has pleaded guilty can appeal against his sentence.

The appellant must give notice of appeal in writing to the clerk of the court and to the prosecutor within fourteen days of the finding. If he fails to serve the notice within this time, Quarter Sessions may waive the irregularity if it thinks fit.

There is no special form of notice. At many courts a printed form is handed to the defendant to complete.

Until the passing of the Criminal Justice Act, 1948, magistrates if they were so minded could prevent a defendant from appealing by fixing the sureties he had to find to prosecute the appeal in such a heavy sum that he could not find them. The Act destroyed this obstacle, and all the appellant has to do now is to give notice of his intention to appeal and to turn up at Quarter Sessions for the hearing.

If he is in custody the magistrates may release him in his own bail or with sureties pending the appeal. Here again the recognizance should be in what the Act describes as a reasonable sum. Should bail be refused by the magistrates or should they require a recognizance that he does not consider reasonable, he may appeal to the High Court both where he is appealing to Quarter Sessions or to the High Court by case stated or for an order of certiorari to remove proceedings from a court of summary jurisdiction into the High Court.

These provisions will of course be of great value to the appellant who has the means to go to the High Court. They ought also, however, to be regarded as a clear indication that the Legislature voicing the feelings of the community is determined that nothing shall be done to prevent an appeal and that whenever possible pending the hearing the appellant is to be released.

These questions of bail and recognizance into which we are constantly running may sometimes seem secondary matters, but they never are for the prisoner. In truth they never are for any of us whilst our fortunes depend upon a State based on law and order. They are the very stuff of our history. To refuse release without the most anxious consideration is to stand with John against Magna Carta and with the Stuarts against the commonweal.

Legal aid may be granted to an appellant from a summary conviction and he may abandon the appeal at any time not less than two clear days of the date fixed for the hearing. If he leaves it later than this he must attend Sessions and take the risks of an unsuccessful appellant; that is, he will be liable to pay the full costs incurred by the respondents, and his sentence may be increased unless the summary court had already imposed upon him the maximum penalty.

In 'appeals by case stated' notice of the intention to appeal must be given within seven days by the dissatisfied party.

The magistrates then 'state the case', which means that they make a concise statement of the facts as they found them after hearing the evidence. They then state what was their decision giving the reasons which led them to it.

This must be done within three months of the application for the case to be stated. In practice the first draft is usually made by the appellant, who then submits it to the respondent for his criticisms. The magistrates make the final copy from this more or less agreed draft and, after signing it, hand it to the appellant who has to forward it to the High Court.

Before the case is handed to the appellant he must enter into a recognizance in a sum fixed by the magistrates to prosecute the appeal without delay. If the appellant is in custody, the recognizance may be conditioned for his release pending the appeal.

In course of time the judges will pronounce upon the decision, either finding no fault with it or sending it back to the magistrates to be altered in the light of their criticisms – sometimes to hear additional evidence and take it into consideration in reaching a decision again, more often to come to a decision opposite to that reached in the summary court.

Occasionally in the past, magistrates have taken these corrections hardly. To kick against the pricks in such a case is not only indecorous. It is dangerous. In dealing with the High Court discretion is very certainly the better part of valour.

CHAPTER 31

POOR PERSONS

THE hackneyed criticism, 'There is one law for the rich and another for the poor' is both superficial and untrue. A cloud of wealthy witnesses who have been roughly handled by the law, of whom the notorious Mr Horatio Bottomley is a representative man, may be called to testify against it. We might as justly say 'There is one law of health for the rich and another for the poor.' Laws are not laws unless they are true for all whether they be laws of science, of hygiene, or of the State.

But the rich score because nearly all their needs being met temptations rarely assail them. 'Millionaires no less than vagabonds are forbidden to sleep under the Paris bridges,' wrote Anatole France. Even if they do succumb to temptation they have another advantage. They can call in the services of the most experienced practitioners to extricate them from their difficulties.

If they need a surgeon they can resign themselves to operation with the comforting reflexion that they have placed themselves in the hands of the best man in the profession. The poor may have to submit to the prentice hand of a raw novice. In law, the contrast may be still more marked. Not only may the poor litigant be unable to obtain the advice of a skilled advocate. He may be able to obtain no advocate at all. He may have to operate himself. Indeed, he often does, and the spectacle to experts who are compelled to witness it but who may not advise him is a distressing one.

So much so that the national conscience has been stirred to the extent of enacting two Poor Prisoners Defence Acts in the present century, the second one of which is an Act of that title passed in 1930.

Regulations provide that 'lists' are to be kept by the Clerks of Assize and Clerks of the Peace at Quarter Sessions of solicitors who are willing to have 'Poor Prisoner' cases assigned to them.

Where the magistrates decide to commit an indictable offence for trial, they may grant the defendant a 'defence certificate' if they think the defendant's means are insufficient to enable him to obtain legal aid and that it is in the interests of justice that he should be so aided. Where the charge is murder, a certificate must be granted if the defendant is without sufficient means. In exceptional cases the assistance of two counsel may be granted.

Magistrates may also grant legal aid to defendants in similar circumstances during the preliminary examination of an indictable offence, or during the trial of a summary offence if they think the case is one of exceptional difficulty. In these cases the magistrates grant a 'legal aid certificate'.

The Summary Jurisdiction (Appeals) Act, 1933, Section 2, allows an 'appeal aid certificate' to be granted to an appellant who has not sufficient means to enable him to obtain legal aid for his appeal.

When any of these certificates is granted, the magistrates assign to the defendant a solicitor whose name appears on one of the 'lists' kept at Assizes or Quarter Sessions. The general practice is to allow the defendant to make his own choice or to select for him a solicitor with an office near the court. A solicitor who is not on the lists cannot have his name added to enable him to take a particular case. To do so would be unfair to those who have announced in advance that they are prepared to take whatever comes along, be it profitable or not.

So far so good. But the magistrates may grant certificates only in those charges where they think it 'desirable in the interests of justice by reason of the gravity of the charge or of exceptional circumstances.' The Act therefore meets the case of the unusually difficult charge, whereas the real problem with which we are faced is that every contested charge, however humdrum and commonplace, calls for scientific handling if the defendant is to have the advantage of the special rules of evidence and procedure designed by our criminal law to protect him. These rules are familiar to the veriest novice in criminal pleading. To most unrepresented defendants they are neither known nor appreciated, and with the best will in the world magistrates may shrink from rushing in to help them.

Take for example the question of character. If a defendant is represented and has not hitherto been convicted his advocate will never let his good character be forgotten. 'My client has never before been charged with any offence of any sort, kind, or description,' he asserts with time-honoured tautology. Yet how rarely does an unrepresented defendant say a word about an unsullied past! How often when the scales are slowly tilting against him could he restore the balance by a challenge to the prosecution with a claim to an unblemished character!

In the face of his silence the magistrates can do nothing. Suppose they take a bold line and point out the value of evidence of good character. In nine cases out of ten they would be safe in doing so, because the defendant in fact would have a good character. But the tenth man would have convictions. If in response to the invitation to speak of his past, he claimed a good character, the prosecution as we saw in Chapter 13 would be able to give evidence of those convictions. If he remained silent or admitted a criminal record, the magistrates would have informed themselves improperly of the man's past and upon appeal would certainly incur the criticism of the judges.

A similar difficulty occurs when calling upon a defendant for his answer to the charge. As we saw in Chapter 11 he may give evidence and may make a statement from the dock. Every advocate, however inexperienced, knows what is implied in these two courses and what critical consequences may flow from them. The unrepresented defendant regards them as distinctions without differences. 'Just as you like,' he answers airily, when told the choice is his and his alone. The court, of course, can explain that if he comes into the witness box he will be sworn and if he tells lies he will be liable to prosecution for perjury; also that he will be subject to cross-examination, but that evidence given under these safeguards will carry greater weight.

But what the unrepresented defendant wants to know is not how these two courses differ but which is the better for him to pursue in the particular circumstances in which he finds himself – to lie low or to come challengingly into the open? For that he needs the advice of an advocate. Conviction or acquittal will often depend upon this fateful decision.

All this is not to criticize what has been done by Parliament to help poor prisoners. It is only to point out the difficulties under which they labour and the need for magistrates who have to try them to appreciate their difficulties and to hear them out in patience and sympathy. Short of providing every unrepresented defendant who contests the charge made against him with an advocate, it is difficult to see what more can be done by Act of Parliament. This would be so expensive that the ratepayer who has to foot the bill may be forgiven if he asks, after paying the constable who has made the arrest, the court expenses, and the fees incurred by the prosecution, whether it would not be cheaper to have no prosecutions at all.

We must remember too what safeguards the law has built up around the prisoner. We saw an outline of them in Chapters 11 to 16 – reasonable doubt, restrictions upon the competency of witnesses and upon what they may say and so on. Standing alone in the dock the unrepresented prisoner looks a forlorn and friendless figure. In fact he is girt about by defences which are none the less real because they are unseen. Protected by them we may reasonably hope that few innocent persons are wrongly convicted. Certain it is that they secure the acquittal of many who are guilty.

So far we have been considering the case of poor prisoners who are resisting the charges made against them. It often happens that a defendant pleads guilty to a charge under a misapprehension of its meaning, a most common example being the confusion which exists in many minds between the meaning of taking and stealing. Less frequently a defendant pleads guilty to a charge when the law provides him with a good defence, sometimes an unanswerable defence. The vigilant bench will be alive to these defences, many of which form fascinating nooks and crannies in our criminal law.

A good illustration of one of these unexpected corners appeared some years ago. A Negro called Hussey rented a room. His landlady wanted to get him out, but, instead of giving him notice in the ordinary way, set herself at the head of a posse of friends and with hammer, spanner, poker, and chisel tried to force the lodger's door. They broke in a panel and the Negro fired through the aperture at his besiegers, wounding two of them. He was committed for trial for unlawful wounding and was sentenced to twelve months hard labour.

Yet to this charge the law had for centuries provided Hussey with a perfect answer. 'In defence of a man's house,' wrote Hale in the days of Cromwell, 'the owner or his family may kill a trespasser who would forcibly dispossess him of it, in the same manner as he might by law kill in self defence a man who attacks him personally; with this distinction, however, that in defending his house he need not retreat, as in other cases of self defence, for that would be giving up his house to his adversary.'

Hussey was defending his house. To retreat was to abandon it to the enemy. The law allowed him to stand firm at whatever cost to his assailants.

But this plea was missed at the summary court in which the preliminary examination took place. It was missed at Assizes where Hussey was convicted and sentenced. Fortunately it was unearthed at the Court of Criminal Appeal, where the conviction was quashed and Hussey set free (*R*. v. *Hussey* (1925), 89 J.P. 28; 18 Cr. App. R. 160).

Hitherto legal aid in the magistrates' courts has been limited to criminal proceedings.

The Legal Aid and Advice Act, 1949, extends legal aid

from public funds to civil proceedings. Persons with an income of less than £420 a year or whose capital does not exceed £500 will be able to apply to a local committee of solicitors and barristers for legal aid. For the summary courts most applications will be made by persons who are parties to domestic proceedings and applications for bastardy orders.

The Act also gives a completely free hand to the magistrates when asked by a defendant to a criminal charge for legal aid.

'If,' says Section 15, 'there is doubt whether his means are sufficient to enable him to obtain legal aid or whether it is desirable in the interests of justice that he should have free legal aid, the doubt shall be resolved in favour of granting him free legal aid.'

Furthermore, the grant of legal aid is not dependent upon 'the gravity of the charge or exceptional circumstances', as was formerly required by the Poor Prisoners' Defence Act, 1930.

CHAPTER 32

CRIME AND THE MIND

EVERY crime consists of physical activity plus mental activity, an act of the body plus an act of the mind – in a few rare cases of a failure or omission to act physically plus an act of mind.

The effect of the mind upon an act is fundamental. To constitute a crime mental activity must always be present. Unseen, intangible, it is far more difficult to assess than the physical activity of which it is the cause. It sets the criminal lawyer his most perplexing problems.

One state of mind will make an act innocent. Another will turn that self-same act into a crime. Yet a third will raise it to a crime of higher degree.

Black picks up a pistol, points it at White, fires it and kills White. Has Black murdered White? Or is he guilty only of manslaughter? Or is he guilty of no crime at all? To answer these questions we must discover what was in Black's mind. The physical activity is the same for all three eventualities.

In all crimes from treason and murder to the pettiest byelaw and regulation, the accused must know at the time he committed the offence; first, that what he did was wrong, and secondly in the case of certain charges the prosecution must prove that he did it with the intent or state of mind needed for the accomplishment of the crime of which he is accused.

To convict Black of murder, for instance, the prosecution must show that he fired at White deliberately and without justification intending to kill him; to convict him of manslaughter, that whilst having no intention of hurting White he behaved with negligence or carelessness. And in both cases Black must have known that what he did was wrong.

But you may say, 'All this may be true enough of murder and manslaughter and crimes that we instinctively feel are wrong, but how can it be said that a man who breaks a bye-law, of the existence of which he had no idea and about which there can be no question of ethics or morals, knows that in so acting he is doing wrong? A motorist, for example, who visiting a town for the first time in his life goes straight on past the statue of Mr Gladstone when a regulation not a week old has decreed that he should turn left and go behind the venerable statesman? How can a motorist in such a case know he is doing wrong?

The law has anticipated this question and has answered it to its own satisfaction if not to our own. It assumes that everyone knows the law. This is not a compliment to our omniscience but purely a measure of self-defence. For if to convict a man of committing a crime the prosecution had to show not only that he had in fact committed it but also that he knew that so to behave was unlawful, the task would be so great that very few persons would be convicted. How show, for example, that the motorist who passed in front of Mr Gladstone knew all about the regulation? Proof would be impossible, for the best of all reasons, that in truth the motorist knew nothing of it. Very sensibly therefore the law does not attempt the impossible. It assumes that the motorist and everyone else knows, or should know, of the existence of the regulation and all other regulations, all bye-laws, orders, and penal sections; and it will not allow us to say we do not.

Now having started from this unreasonable premise, the law proceeds to a simple logical deduction. Since you know all criminal offences in existence, it argues, then you must know it is wrong to commit them. Thus is imported that awareness of wrong which is necessary in all crimes of low no less than high degree.

There is only one defence an accused person can make to this assumption – the defence of insanity. An insane person cannot know the difference between right and wrong. Such a defence can be made to all criminal charges, but is in practice made only to the most serious, because if successful the offender may be detained in a criminal lunatic asylum during Her Majesty's pleasure.

This mental activity which must be present in the commission of every crime is called by lawyers the 'mens rea'. Literally translated the words mean 'guilty mind', but the phrase is not used to mean a sense of shame or guilt at having committed an offence, as this literal translation would imply. It means that the court must be satisfied that at the time the offender committed the physical act forming part of the crime he was also guilty of the mental activity necessary to commit the crime, or at least doing what he knew was unlawful.

In all crimes this last low degree of mental activity must be present. In the more serious crimes not only this low degree must be present but in addition the higher degree of deliberate intention.

Thus in the 'Gladstone' regulation we have used as an illustration the lower degree of 'mens rea' must be present but not necessarily the higher. This is true and typical of the great majority of summary offences, but in nearly all indictable offences and many of the more serious summary offences the higher degree is also demanded.

This brings us to two practical questions – how can the prosecution prove the existence of a guilty mind, seeing that nobody can say what is going on inside another person's mind? And how can we know in which crimes intention or mental activity must be proved?

'The thought of man is not triable,' said a medieval judge, 'for the devil himself knoweth not the thought of man.' To this a later judge retorted, 'The state of a man's mind is as much a fact as the state of his digestion.' We can discover what was the state of a defendant's mind by his actions preceding the commission of a physical act, during it, and after it – by the evidence of preparations, for example, by threats, by statements made by him, by attempts to conceal what he has done. Sometimes it can be proved by showing that the same thing has happened before and what would by itself look like an accident or a mistake is in truth something very different. Poor Smith finding his bride drowned in her bath has all our sympathy. But assured that some half-dozen other brides lost their lives in similar circumstances, we do not hesitate to take our stand with the jury who send poor Smith to the gallows.

Then how can we know in which crimes intention or mental activity must be positively proved?

In most cases by reading the section, regulation, or bye-law which makes an act a crime. As a general rule, if we find no words indicating that the act must be done wilfully or deliberately, then the prosecution will have finished its task upon mere proof that the act has been committed.

The Road Traffic Act, 1934, Section 1, for instance, provides that 'it shall not be lawful for any person to drive a motor vehicle on a road in a built-up area at a speed exceeding thirty miles per hour.' There are no words here to indicate that the offence must be committed intentionally or knowingly, and hence the motorist who exceeds the limit inadvertently is equally liable with the driver who does so deliberately, though, of course, the magistrates can differentiate between them in assessing the penalty.

As we have said, offences in which the higher degree of mens rea need not be proved are usually petty summary offences for which only a fine may be imposed in the first instance, but we cannot make this a rule of practice because there are a number of summary offences for which imprisonment without the option can be inflicted and yet the higher degree of guilty intent need not be present. Sections 11 and 15 of the Road Traffic Act, 1930, which make 'dangerous driving' and 'driving when under the influence of drink' offences contain no words indicating that the court must find that a defendant charged with committing these offences must have done so 'knowingly' or 'intentionally'. From the viewpoint of mens rea these very serious offences are on the same low level as 'exceeding the speed limit' and the 'Gladstone' regulation.

Common examples of words importing the higher degree of mens rea are 'wilfully', 'knowingly', 'with intent to deceive or defraud'.

A difficult word is 'permit'. It occurs frequently in summary offences and the layman is puzzled by it because he generally gives it a narrower meaning than the lawyer. 'To permit' means to him 'to authorize' or 'to give permission'. A car owner is summoned for permitting a friend to drive his car. The friend has no licence to drive and the user was therefore not covered by insurance. 'Permit' seems to the owner in such cases to be limited to the permission to take the car; but Mr Justice Humphreys has defined the legal meaning of the term as 'a failure to take proper steps to prevent' the commission of an offence. The charge thus paraphrased would read 'Brown failed to take proper steps to prevent Green from using his car when Green's user was not covered by a policy of insurance' (*Churchill* v. *Norris* (1938), 158 L.T. 255).

On the other hand the owner will not be held liable for 'permitting' if the borrower uses the car lawfully in a way which the owner could not reasonably foresee – as, for example, if he exceeds the speed limit or drives whilst under the influence of drink.

Sometimes the criminal intention and the physical act are combined in a single word or phrase – as, for example, 'to assault' or 'to steal', 'to rob' or 'to murder'. Such expressions are generally used correctly even in everyday speech. When we say 'he was knocked down', we mean something very different from 'he was assaulted'; 'he died' from 'he was murdered'; 'it was taken' from 'it was stolen'; and the difference in each case is that the second expression imports a criminal intent.

Even in slang these differences are sharply maintained. 'My aunt died of influenza: so they said,' observed Eliza Doolittle when making her first afternoon call. 'But it's my belief they done the old woman in.' The delighted audience is in no doubt about the meaning of 'done her in'.

Probably for this reason common and well understood terms summing up a criminal offence in a word or phrase are often not defined by the Act of Parliament which created them. There is, for example, no definition of assault in the statutes. The great Larceny Act of 1861 did not contain a definition of stealing. On the other hand the Larceny Act, 1916, which largely superseded it, devoted its very first section to one; very comprehensive it is, and one which should be carefully studied whenever questions of mens rea arise upon charges of stealing.

Definitions of offences are a much more common feature of modern Acts of Parliament than they used to be. It is well that they are, because the common understanding of a word denoting a crime can be misleading and incomplete as often as it is apt and accurate. Thus most people would define bigamy as 'to go through a form of marriage with another when the lawful spouse is still alive'; and, indeed, the Offences against the Person Act, 1861, Section 57, under which criminal proceedings are taken uses much the same terms – 'Whoever, being married, shall marry any other person during the life of the former husband or wife.' Here we have an offence designated in an Act of Parliament but no word or phrase to indicate whether a guilty intention is needed to commit the offence or not.

The statute itself provides a defence where a spouse has not been heard of for seven years, but suppose, for example, a wife has excellent reasons for thinking her husband is dead less than seven years after the marriage? Is it bigamy if she marries again and later the husband returns? Thus in the eighteen-eighties, Mrs Tolson's husband was on a ship which sank in the Atlantic – it was thought with all hands. Mrs Tolson had every reason to think that her husband had gone down with the ship. She married again and in due course back came Mr Tolson, like the hero of one of the three-decker novels so popular at the time. Mrs Tolson was convicted of bigamy, but upon appeal the conviction was quashed, the judges holding that in all charges of such magnitude and antiquity as this, a guilty intent is essential, though the Act describing the offence has no phrase or word to indicate that such an intent is needed (*R.* v. *Tolson* (1889), 23 Q.B.D. 168).

So where we can get no guidance in reading the Act or regulation creating an offence, it may be that the question will have been answered by the judges in a case they have decided. Of these, *R.* v. *Tolson* is a striking example.

CHAPTER 33

THE MIND DISEASED

In the last chapter we considered the relationship between the criminal law and the sane.

How do the criminal courts deal with the insane and mentally defective?

The defence of insanity according to strict legal procedure can be raised only by the defendant – usually it is put forward by his representative. In minor summary charges the defendant is often unrepresented and the first indication that the magistrates get that the prisoner is 'queer' may be a hint from the police or a sample of the defendant's eccentric behaviour in court. In such circumstances the general practice is to discontinue the proceedings and remand the accused in custody for examination by the prison doctor. If when the defendant again appears in court the doctor indicates that in his opinion the defendant is insane, he is discharged and taken off to an asylum – in pursuance of the Lunacy Act, 1890, s. 20, which allows a constable to take him straight off to what was then the workhouse and is now the institution, where he can be detained as long as three days to enable a justice in lunacy to make the necessary investigation.

The Magistrates' Courts Act, 1952, Section 30, now allows magistrates to make a reception order themselves whenever a person is charged with any offence for which they can impose imprisonment and are 'satisfied on the evidence of at least two duly qualified medical practitioners that the person is of unsound mind and are also satisfied that he is a proper person to be detained.'

The section is so worded that it applies to indictable offences triable summarily as well as to summary offences, and the magistrates do not require the defendant's consent to their jurisdiction before acting under it. The phrasing may be compared to the Trial of Lunatics Act, 1883, which empowers a jury to bring in a special verdict of 'guilty of the act but so insane as not to be responsible, according to law, for his actions at the time when the act was done.' Under s. 30 of the Magistrates' Courts Act too the magistrates must be satisfied that 'the act or omission charged' has been committed before they can proceed to make an order.

This divorce of act from intention must be a painful expedient for the legal purist, but the section provides a good practical way of dealing with a difficult problem.

When a prisoner is charged with an Indictable Offence which is not triable summarily, he must be committed for trial, when the defendant himself or his representatives can plead insanity or he can be dealt with under the Trial of Lunatics Act, 1883, or other Acts which apply only to proceedings at Assizes and Quarter Sessions.

In some cases, of course, the prosecution may ask even now that the magistrates should commit a defendant for trial instead of dealing with him under the Magistrates' Courts Act, because it may be desirable that he should be treated as a criminal lunatic and placed under greater restraint than is normally the lot of those detained pursuant to the Lunacy Act, 1890.

Sometimes the defence elects to be dealt with summarily and then attempts to contest the charge by setting up a plea of insanity as though it were a defence of fact. We commonly meet with the phenomenon in shop-lifting cases. The defendant is said to have been seized with 'a fit of kleptomania' or to have been impelled by an 'uncontrollable impulse'. These defences are in reality pleas of insanity. Magistrates should refuse to try the charges in which they are raised and insist upon committing. At Assizes and Quarter Sessions it is very unlikely that anything will be heard of the 'uncontrollable impulse', because if successful such a defence may end in the defendant's detention in a criminal lunatic asylum for an indefinite period.

Midway between the sane and the insane are the mentally deficient. The Mental Deficiency Act, 1927, s. 1, divides them into four groups – idiots, imbeciles, feeble-minded persons, and moral defectives – and defines them carefully.

The criminal law holds the defectives who come into the last two groups as responsible for their actions as the sane but allows the courts upon finding them guilty of an offence punishable in the case of an adult with penal servitude or imprisonment to send them to an institution for the care of the mentally deficient instead of dealing with them as they would with normal prisoners.

After conviction if the court has any reason to believe that a defendant comes into one of the categories of the mentally deficient the usual practice is to remand him for examination by a prison doctor. If he considers that the defendant is certifiable as a defective, the magistrates remand him again for examination by a doctor of the County Council, which will have to maintain him if he is eventually found to be certifiable. This doctor attends at the next hearing and if he considers the accused to be defective he must say so on oath and give his reasons. The defendant can oppose his findings, can give evidence, and call witnesses to show that he is not defective. If he fails in this, the court may make an order that he be detained in an institution for the mentally deficient.

Yet another group of delinquents – perhaps the largest of all – suffer from some mental trouble which does not bring them into any of the recognized categories of mental deficiency and yet are greatly in need of some kind of mental treatment if delinquency in the future is to be avoided. The Criminal Justice Act, 1948, s. 4, now allows the courts to make it a condition of a probation order that the offender shall 'submit, for a period not exceeding twelve months, to treatment by or under the direction of a duly qualified medical practitioner with a view to the improvement of his mental condition.'

The provision is subject to very careful regulation and, of course, can be employed only with the defendant's consent.

CHAPTER 34

CIVIL PROCEEDINGS

WE considered the chief differences which exist between criminal and civil proceedings in Chapter 7. We saw too the key words which indicate that proceedings are civil – a 'complaint' by a 'complainant' to the magistrates to make an 'order' as opposed in the case of criminal proceedings to an 'information' by a 'prosecutor' or 'informant' to obtain a 'finding of guilt' or a 'conviction'.

Several times in describing the work of the magistrates dealing with crime we have characterized the summary courts as criminal clearing houses. They have no such function in dealing with civil matters. They have nothing to do with the preliminary stages of actions which are to be tried in the High Court or in the County Courts. Civil proceedings which begin in the summary courts end in them and no question of the defendants' consenting to jurisdiction arises as we have seen it constantly does during the proceedings in criminal charges.

Procedure generally is very similar to the procedure followed in the trial of a summary offence. The Magistrates' Courts Act, 1952, is the basis of both. The rules for the service of summonses are the same. In court, witnesses are sworn, they must not be led, and they must give evidence only of what they themselves have sensed. The defendant, however, is not in the protected position he is in when he is the defendant to a criminal charge. In a civil complaint he may be called as a witness by the complainant and so may his wife. His character too may be attacked whether or not an attack has been made upon the character of the complainant. In practice these tactics are rarely employed because they are not encouraged by the magistrates. 'I can't shut this out,' the chairman of one bench used to observe upon such occasions, 'but I can say it is having the opposite effect upon me to that which is presumably intended.'

Some Acts to a greater or lesser extent regulate their own procedure. These are notably the Distress for Rates Act, 1849, under which the magistrates enforce the payment of rates, the Bastardy Acts, and the Married Women (Summary Jurisdiction) Acts. Where these Acts are silent upon particular questions of procedure, the Magistrates' Courts Act, 1952, fills the gap.

Where an Act gives the magistrates power to make an order without adding how it is to be enforced the procedure is regulated by the Magistrates' Courts Act, 1952, Section 54. The defendant may be ordered to pay £1 for every day during which he has failed to comply with the order or to be imprisoned until he has remedied his default. This sum must not exceed £20 and the period of imprisonment must not be longer than two months.

There is no general right of appeal to Quarter Sessions against the making of a civil order as there is a general right of appeal against a conviction or a finding of guilt upon a charge. To discover if there is a right of appeal we must look at the Act which gives the magistrates the right to make a particular order. If nothing is said about a right of appeal we must conclude that none exists. The Dogs Act, 1871, for instance, allows magistrates to make an order for the destruction of a dog they consider to be dangerous. There was no right of appeal against the exercise of this drastic power until it was belatedly given by the Dogs (Amendment) Act, 1938.

On the other hand, either of the parties in civil proceedings can appeal to the Divisional Court by case stated on the ground that the magistrates have acted erroneously in point of law or in excess of jurisdiction.

CHAPTER 35

CIVIL DEBTS

ONLY favoured creditors are allowed to pursue their debtors in the summary courts. Tradesmen would no doubt be very glad to do so before the local bench sitting perhaps as frequently as twice a month instead of having to wait for the County Court, which may mean a journey to a distant town and a delay of six or eight weeks.

These favoured creditors are permitted to proceed in the summary courts by Act of Parliament. Among them are Her Majesty's Collector of Taxes, who may take summary proceedings up to any amount for arrears due from manual workers and up to £50 for arrears due upon a half-yearly assessment for other classes of income tax-payers; water, gas, electricity, and other public utility undertakings, which usually have the foresight to include in the Act of Parliament by which they live and have their being a section giving them the right to take proceedings for arrears summarily; local authorities which incur expense in maintaining old or invalid persons under the Poor Law Acts and which can compel relatives to share the cost.

It is the duty of the debtor to seek out his creditor. Jurisdiction for these complaints is therefore not the area in which the debtor lives but the area in which payment should be made – usually the office of the Tax Collector or of the public undertaking or of the local authority.

Proceedings must be commenced within six months of the demand for payment. If the debtor makes a payment within this period, the time limit will begin to run afresh from the date on which part payment is made.

The creditor begins with a complaint that a given sum is due to him. The debtor is summoned to appear on a specified day. If the summons is not served, nothing more can be done until the defendant's whereabouts are discovered. A warrant cannot be issued for his arrest. In most cases the summons is served but the debtor does not attend. Unless he has paid beforehand, the court makes an order in default. If he does attend and disputes that he owes the debt the complainant must seek to prove that he does.

When the order is made, a 'minute' of the order must be served upon the debtor to notify him of its existence. Once served the creditor can at any time ask the court to issue a distress warrant to be levied on the defendant's goods or he can ask for a judgement summons.

At the hearing of the judgement summons, the creditor must show that his debtor has the means to pay his debt or has had them since the making of the order. To prove this he may call the defendant as a witness. He may also call his employer or any person who can give evidence of any wages or payments made to the defendant; or without calling any witness at all he can put in as prima facie evidence a statement signed by or on behalf of the defendant's employer to show what wages have been paid to him.

If the magistrates find that the debtor could have paid had he honestly wished, they may now order him to pay what is due or to go to prison. The limit of imprisonment is six weeks, set by Paragraph 4 of the Third Schedule of the Magistrates' Courts Act, 1952. The scale fixed by the same schedule must also be observed.

Once the debtor has undergone a term of imprisonment he cannot again be sent to prison for the same debt, but if he comes into possession of property he can be distrained upon for the debt, notwithstanding that he has been imprisoned.

CHAPTER 36

RATES

THE rate collector like the Collector of Taxes is also privileged to pursue his defaulters in the magistrates' courts. His Act of Parliament is the Distress for Rates Act, 1849.

Upon proof that the rate has been duly levied, that the ratepayer has been properly assessed and has failed to pay the amount due from him, the magistrates may make an order that he is to pay or in default a distress may be levied on his goods.

Up to 1935 if the defaulter had no goods upon which distress could be levied, he could be sent to prison forthwith for any time up to three months. This is not subject to the scale laid down by the Magistrates' Courts Act, 1952, Third Schedule (see page 109). The Money Payments (Justices Procedure) Act of that year has put an end to the power of immediate committal. Before an order of committal to prison can now be made, the magistrates must summon the defaulter for an enquiry into his means to determine in his presence whether 'his failure to pay . . . is due either to his wilful refusal or culpable neglect.' If he fails to appear a warrant must be issued to compel him to do so. If the magistrates find that the failure to pay is due to no fault of the debtor the warrant must not be issued.

In suitable cases the magistrates may remit part or the whole of the sum due.

Rates are intended to be paid by the person who enjoys the benefits of the services for which they are levied – the police who guard the premises, the street lamps which light the way to them, the water and sanitary services which are brought to the door.

This is known as the beneficial use of premises, which constitutes occupation for the purpose of rating. The term was well explained in *R.* v. *St Pancras Assessment Committee* (1877), Q.B., by Mr Justice Lush.

'So long as an owner leaves a house vacant, he is not rateable. If, however, he furnishes it, and keeps it ready for habitation whenever he pleases to go to it, he is an occupier, though he may not reside in it one day in a year. On the other hand, a person who, without having any title, takes actual possession of a house or piece of land, whether by leave of the owner or against his will, is the occupier of it. Another element, however, besides actual possession of the land, is necessary to constitute the kind of occupation which the Act contemplates, and that is permanence. An itinerant showman who erects a temporary structure for his performance may be in exclusive, actual possession, and may, with strict grammatical propriety, be said to occupy the ground on which the structure is placed, but it is clear that he is not such an occupier as the statute intends.'

To this we may add that where a caretaker is put in to look after a house until it is sold or let, neither the owner nor the caretaker is rateable.

A common defence to a summons for rates is made by a tenant occupier who says that his landlord should pay them. This, of course, is a matter the landlord and tenant must fight out between them. As far as the rating authority and the courts are concerned, the occupier is the person responsible for them.

For certain classes of property the rating authority may, by resolution, direct that the owners instead of the occupiers shall be rated.

CHAPTER 37

HUSBAND AND WIFE

THERE is a popular superstition which will probably endure as long as Justices of the Peace themselves that magistrates have a sovereign specific which is a remedy against all the ills a wife can suffer at the hands of her husband. This specific is known as a Protection Order – sometimes affectionately as a 'Protection'. Although such an order is unknown to magisterial law to-day, wives go on asking for it at a busy court at the rate of about four per week. Furthermore they appear to think it can be granted upon application as readily as a doctor writes out a medical certificate, and once obtained will unfailingly frighten the husband into better ways. The magistrates certainly have been entrusted with great powers to protect one spouse from the misconduct of another and to compel a husband who is not maintaining his family to do so. But they are not so summary and informal as this.

As in the juvenile courts, the benches dealing with these complaints are now composed of not more than three justices and as far as possible both sexes are represented. The general public are not admitted to the sittings. Press representatives must be allowed to attend, though their reports are severely curtailed by Section 58 of the Magistrates' Courts Act, 1952. To encourage a friendly and conciliatory attitude, the proceedings may be as informal as is consistent with a fair and legal hearing.

The basis of the magistrates' powers to make separation or maintenance orders is the Summary Jurisdiction (Married Women) Act, 1895. As a glance at the Act will show, these proceedings were primarily devised as a quick and handy remedy for poor women who could not take their grievances into the Divorce Court.

Section 4 of the Act sets out certain grounds upon which proceedings can be taken by a wife against a violent or

irresponsible husband. These grounds, extended as we shall
see by later Acts, cover a wide field, so wide that it might be
thought they meet every form of matrimonial complaint of
any substance. In practice it will be found that not infre-
quently a case arises which does not come within any of
the grounds set out in the Acts. When this happens the
magistrates should refuse to make an order, however much
they may sympathize with the complainant – possibly with
both parties.

Since 1895, for example, probably some thousands of
orders have been made ostensibly on a ground to be found
in the statutes but in reality on the ground that 'the parties
are living a cat and dog life' –as good a reason, it must be
admitted, as any other for separating an ill-matched pair
except that no Act so far has empowered the summary
courts to base an order upon it.

Wives, of course, are enormously in the majority in
applying for these orders. A summons should not be granted
too readily. If the complaint upon the hearing turns out to
be insubstantial the wife will not get an order and the proceedings are unlikely to improve already strained relations.
It is both good practice and good sense to point out to the
wife the limitations of an order. She may bring her husband
to court but often it will be found she cannot make him pay.
The order may turn him into the most determined passive
resister paying only when summoned for arrears and not
then if the magistrates are infirm of purpose. Even if the
husband pays with commendable regularity his earnings will
usually be insufficient to maintain two separate establish-
ments. From every point of view the wife will be well advised
to let the court missionary try his hand at reconciliation
before the court acts at all. If, however, she makes out a case
for a summons and refuses to entertain any attempt
at conciliation, her application cannot rightfully be
denied.

The grounds upon which orders may be made upon the
application of the wife are as follows:

MC–8

The Summary Jurisdiction (Married Women) Act, 1895, Section 4, provides five grounds:

1. Her husband has been convicted summarily of an aggravated assault upon her within the meaning of the Offences against the Person Act, 1861, Section 43.

After hearing the evidence upon a charge of common assault upon a wife or child, the justices may consider the case such a bad one that their ordinary powers of punishment – two months imprisonment or a fine of £5 – are insufficient. They may then hold that the assault is an aggravated assault punishable by imprisonment up to six months.

Where the assault is by a husband upon his wife the magistrates, in addition to or instead of any punishment they may inflict, may make orders of separation or maintenance. A summons may be issued immediately after conviction but the husband should be told that he can have an adjournment if he wishes.

2. Her husband has been convicted upon indictment of an assault upon her, and sentenced to pay a fine of more than £5 or to a term of imprisonment exceeding two months.

The orders may be made at the Assize or Quarter Sessions where the husband is convicted or later at a court of summary jurisdiction.

3. Her husband has deserted her.

A husband may be said to have deserted his wife when he leaves her against her will without good reason. Many years ago a judge defined desertion in more exact language as 'actually and wilfully bringing to an end an existing state of cohabitation without the consent of the other spouse and without just and reasonable cause' (*Fitzgerald* v. *Fitzgerald* (1869), L.R.I.P. & D. 694).

The husband may leave his wife by quitting the home himself or constructively by compelling his wife to go. It may even be sufficient if he shuts himself away from her in one part of the house, for in doing so he puts an end to their cohabitation.

'Cohabitation' to lawyers has a special meaning. It means

living together as man and wife as far as circumstances permit. Thus the members of a family reside with each other but only the parents cohabit. On the other hand, a soldier is considered to be still cohabiting with his wife though he may be abroad on active service and she left behind in England.

The husband must leave his wife against her will. If the parties separate by mutual agreement – for example, by private deed – the wife cannot afterwards complain of desertion. She agreed to her husband's going as he agreed to hers. She may sometimes, however, obtain an order on the ground of 'wilful neglect to maintain'.

Good reason for the husband to leave his wife would be her adultery, but it may include 'conduct falling short of a matrimonial offence'. The good reason, however, must always be 'grave and weighty'. A conviction for larceny, frailty of temper, and distasteful habits has been held to be insufficient. The judges have decided many cases on this point.

A husband can put an end to his desertion if he makes a bona fide offer to resume cohabitation. If the wife refuses to accept the offer she can no longer continue with her application. The offer is often made to defeat a complaint and magistrates should be on their guard against taking at their face value what may be no more than impudent tactics to silence a well-founded claim.

4. Her husband has been guilty of persistent cruelty to her.

'Cruelty' has been defined as such as to 'inflict bodily injury upon the wife, or cause reasonable apprehension of suffering or injury to her health.'

There may be mental cruelty as well as physical. In one case the judges held that where a husband brought another woman into the house, committed adultery with her, and compelled his wife to wait upon her, this amounted to persistent cruelty.

One act of cruelty, however aggravated, is not sufficient

to establish persistent cruelty. In a few rare cases an order has been made where the cruelty of which the wife complained all took place on one day, but generally the court looks for evidence of a series of incidents spread over a period.

5. Her husband has wilfully neglected to provide reasonable maintenance for her or her infant children whom he is legally liable to maintain.

The wife must show that the husband has had the means to support her and has wilfully failed to do so. The maintenance that the wife demands must be reasonable having regard to the husband's earnings.

The wife is not entitled to an order if she has failed to fulfil her part of the matrimonial contract. If she leaves her husband without good cause or has unreasonably refused him marital rights, she has no grounds for complaint.

If the husband falls into arrears under a deed of separation, the wife can enforce payment only in the County Court. As a general rule the deed, being the record of a mutual agreement to part, will debar her from obtaining a separation or maintenance order later. But if she can show that the husband has failed to pay under the deed when he could have done so, the Judges have in recent years held that the wife may obtain an order for 'wilful neglect' (*McCreaney* v. *McCreaney* (1928), 92 J.P. 44).

A sixth ground was added by the Licensing Act, 1902, Section 5 (1).

6. Her husband is an habitual drunkard.

The Habitual Drunkards Act, 1879, Section 3, defines the habitual drunkard as 'A person who, not being amenable to any jurisdiction in lunacy, is, notwithstanding, by reason of habitual intemperate drinking of intoxicating liquor, at times dangerous to himself or to others, or incapable of managing himself and his affairs'.

By the Summary Jurisdiction (Separation and Maintenance) Act, 1925, Section 3, the definition is now to be read as if it included 'a reference to the habitual taking or using, except upon medical advice, of opium or other dangerous drugs within the meaning of the Dangerous Drugs Acts, 1920 and 1923'.

The Summary Jurisdiction (Separation and Maintenance) Act, 1925, Section 1 (2), gave the wife three more grounds:

7. Her husband has been guilty of persistent cruelty to her children.

8. Her husband while suffering from a venereal disease, and knowing that he was so suffering, insisted on having sexual intercourse with her.

9. Her husband has compelled her to submit herself to prostitution.

Finally the Matrimonial Causes Act, 1937, Section 11, gives a tenth ground:

10. Her husband has been guilty of adultery.

Proceedings instituted in consequence of adultery are subject to an important rule of evidence designed to protect both the parties to the proceedings and their witnesses and no doubt owing its origin to times when to be found guilty of adultery brought consequences in its train as dire as a conviction of a serious crime. No one can be asked in the course of these proceedings if he has committed adultery unless he has first given evidence denying such conduct.

In bastardy proceedings the mother may call the defendant to corroborate her evidence that he is the father of her child. A wife complaining of her husband's adultery cannot take a similar course. He can be called as her witness for other complaints – neglect, cruelty, and so on – but he must not be asked if he has committed adultery unless he voluntarily admits or denies it. In other words the complainant in contested proceedings for adultery whether husband or wife must produce evidence sufficient to establish the complaint without being able to rely upon the accused spouse.

An application may be made by the husband on three grounds:

1. His wife is an habitual drunkard, Licensing Act, 1902, Section 5 (2).

2. His wife has been guilty of persistent cruelty to his children, Summary Jurisdiction (Separation and Maintenance) Act, 1925, Section 1 (3).

3. His wife has been guilty of adultery, Matrimonial Causes Act, 1937, Section 11.

Before magistrates the husband cannot apply for an order on the ground of his wife's desertion, but he can do so in the Divorce Court.

The procedure followed to obtain an order is similar to that for other complaints and is generally upon the lines laid down in the Summary Jurisdiction Acts.

The time limit of six months applies to complaints based on assaults and persistent cruelty – in the latter the limit is calculated from the date of the last act of cruelty. Desertion and neglect to maintain are 'continuing courses of conduct' similar to 'continuing offences' and the limit begins to operate only from the moment they cease. A complaint based on adultery is subject to the limit (*Teall* v. *Teall* [1938], P. 250).

By virtue of the Married Women (Maintenance) Act, 1949, Section 6, proceedings can now be taken not only in the district in which the cause of complaint has wholly or partly arisen but also in that 'in which the married woman or her husband ordinarily resides.'

The same Act by Section 5 allows the magistrates to make such provision as they think fit for access to the children of the marriage by the husband or wife when they make an order with regard to the custody of the children.

If the husband does not appear to answer the complaint, the proceedings are usually adjourned to give him another opportunity to attend. Should he then default the complaint is usually heard in his absence after proof that the summons has been served. If the magistrates think it desirable they can compel his attendance on proof that the summons has been served by issuing a warrant, but this is rarely done. All this, of course, applies equally to a wife when she is the defendant.

In many cases the only witnesses are the couple them-selves. Corroboration is not essential upon any ground, but where the parties could support their evidence by calling witnesses they should be required to do so. It is no light matter to dub either spouse with the character implied in any one of the grounds upon which an order must be founded. Where the accused strongly contests the allegations of the complainant, the magistrates should safeguard themselves against coming to a wrong decision by casting about for witnesses who may have been present when some of the acts complained of were committed or who have seen some of their consequences – a wife's black eye, for example.

Cases frequently occur which turn upon the intimate incidents of married life. Here the magistrates can look to no independent witness for guidance but have to decide between the conflicting stories of the husband and wife. A case illustrating such an impasse is referred to in Chapter 7 at page 42 with Lord Birkenhead's comments upon it.

Not only at the beginning but all through the proceedings the magistrates may rightly urge upon the parties the wisdom of making a fresh start in their matrimonial venture. Elaborate machinery to this end has been set up by Section 59 of the Magistrates' Courts Act, 1952.

If the magistrates feel that time may mend matters they may adjourn the complaint and make an Interim Order under which meantime the husband will be ordered to pay his wife a weekly sum for maintenance. The order cannot be made for an adjournment of a week or less nor for more than three months.

If the magistrates eventually come to the conclusion that the complaint has been made out, they are empowered by the Summary Jurisdiction (Married Women) Act, 1895, to make one or more of the following orders:

1. That the wife be no longer bound to cohabit with her husband.

This is a 'Separation Order'. The term is used to distinguish it from an order of maintenance (see 3 below) unaccompanied by this non-cohabitation clause. An order without it is popularly termed a 'Maintenance Order'.

Separation Orders are rarely made now except where the wife is in fear of violence or molestation from her husband. In the absence of these reasons the judges have strongly condemned the making of this order.

2. That the legal custody of any children of the marriage while under sixteen be committed to the wife.

The children are generally entrusted to the wife, unless the magistrates think she is unfitted for the responsibility. In all cases the paramount consideration is the welfare of the children. If they are given to the wife, the husband may be ordered to pay a weekly sum not exceeding thirty shillings for each child in addition to the sum he is ordered to pay his wife.

3. That the husband shall pay to his wife personally or for her use to any officer of the court or third person on her behalf such weekly sum not exceeding five pounds as the court shall, having regard to the means both of the husband and wife, consider reasonable.

4. That either of the parties shall pay the costs of the proceedings.

Section 6 of the Act of 1895 prohibited the making of any of these orders 'if it shall be proved that such married woman has committed an act of adultery; provided that the husband has not condoned, or connived at, or by his wilful neglect or misconduct conduced to such act of adultery.'

But the following section of the Act allowed the wife no excuse if she committed adultery after the making of a Maintenance Order – 'If any married woman shall commit an act of adultery such order shall upon proof thereof be discharged.'

The Act recognizes that there may be an excuse for a wife who commits adultery where the husband is to some extent responsible for her misconduct, but once an order was made, no lapse could be excused. The wife now had her remedy and the Act took no account of the possibility that a husband might deliberately abstain from paying an order in the hope that his wife might be compelled to maintain herself by immorality and thus provide him with a ready means of putting an end to the order. The Summary Jurisdiction (Separation and Maintenance) Act, 1925, Section 2 (1), modifies the rigidity of the earlier Act by providing that the court may 'refuse to discharge the order if, in its opinion, such act of adultery was conduced to by the failure of the husband to make such payments as in the opinion of the court he was able to make. '

Neither in proceedings under Section 6 nor Section 7 does the time limit of six months apply where a husband sets up the defence that his wife has committed adultery (*Natborny* v. *Natborny* [1933], P. 1). The six months' limit is a bar only where one of the spouses seeks to obtain a new order on that ground. Then the complaint must be that the adultery or some part of it took place within six months of the application for a summons.

If the order is discharged, the wife may still be allowed to keep the children and a new order may be made that the husband pay a weekly sum for their maintenance not exceeding ten shillings per week for each child.

Appeals against orders made under these Acts and against refusals to make orders are heard in the Divorce Division of the High Court.

After an order has been made either spouse may by summons ask for it to be varied. Usually the variation asked for is upon the ground of increasing or diminishing incomes.

If the husband falls into arrear, the wife may seek to enforce the order by applying for a summons. If the husband fails to appear upon this a warrant may be granted. In their discretion, the magistrates may issue a warrant instead of a summons. But nothing can be done to enforce the order until the attendance of the husband has been secured, because upon these proceedings he is liable to imprisonment forthwith.

Upon proof that the arrears are due, payment may be enforced by distress upon the husband's property – only rarely has he any – or by imprisonment up to three months subject to the scale laid down by the Magistrates' Courts Act, 1952, Third Schedule; but since the Money Payments (Justices Procedure) Act, 1935, Section 8, a husband cannot be sent to prison forthwith unless the magistrates are satisfied that his failure has been due to his 'wilful refusal or culpable neglect' to pay the order.

The same section allows the court to remit the whole or part of the arrears in appropriate cases.

Where a wife is unable or unwilling to obtain orders under the Summary Jurisdiction Act, 1895, she may apply for an order under the Guardianship of Infants Act, 1925, for an order giving her the custody of the children of the marriage. Maintenance may be allowed under the Act up to thirty shillings weekly.

A wife whose husband has gone to the Dominions or colonies may still hope for some financial support from him by virtue of the Maintenance Orders (Facilities for Enforcement) Act, 1920. The Act applies to most parts of the Empire except some provinces of Canada. Orders already in existence before the husband's departure may be registered by the appropriate court in the country to which he has gone. If no order was in existence, a provisional order may be made and sent abroad for confirmation. Reciprocal legislation allows the Empire to send orders here for registration and confirmation.

By the Maintenance Orders Act, 1950, Section 1, a wife residing in England can proceed against a husband residing in Scotland or Northern Ireland if the parties 'last ordinarily resided together as man and wife in England.'

An order so made is registered in Scotland or Northern Ireland and enforced by the authorities of those countries.

CHAPTER 38

BASTARDY PROCEEDINGS

THE object of bastardy proceedings is purely matter-of-fact. It is not to show up the father nor to provide an opportunity for a running commentary upon what young people are coming to nowadays. Their prosaic purpose is to keep the luckless infant off the rates. And so an application for a summons to obtain a bastardy order may be made not only by the mother but also by a County Council if the child becomes chargeable.

The mother may make the application to any court within whose jurisdiction she happens to be, but she must not take up residence in a district rather than in the area in which she has hitherto resided solely for the purpose of obtaining an order there. To allow this would be tantamount to permitting her to choose her own court. A bench with a reputation for being more favourably disposed towards the woman than its neighbours might find itself dealing with all the applications of a county.

Affiliation proceedings are based on the Bastardy Laws Amendment Act, 1872. Section 3 of the Act provides that 'any single woman' may make an application. The term 'single woman' has been explained by the judges in a number of decisions. They are another excellent example of how our English case law system works. Is a widow a single woman? The judges have held she is. A married woman separated by court order from her husband? Again the judges held she is. A married woman still cohabiting within the legal meaning of the term with her husband but separated from him for a long period – a woman, for example, whose husband is serving a long term of imprisonment or who is abroad on foreign station? Again the judges held that such a woman came within the meaning of the phrase. On the other hand, they held that a woman who makes an application after marrying is no longer 'a single woman' and is debarred even if she took out the summons before she was married.

The application must be made within twelve months of the birth of the child. If, however, the alleged or putative father, as the Bastardy Acts call him, has paid money for the maintenance of the child within the first twelve months of its life, the application can be made at any time. Again if the putative father leaves the country so that a summons cannot be served upon him, the application can be made at any time within twelve months of his return.

If the mother wishes she may make the application before the child is born. Her object in doing so is to ensure the payment of maintenance from the birth of the child. If the application is made within two months of the birth the magistrates may order that maintenance be paid from the day the child was born. Sometimes as a result of the confinement the mother is unable to make her application within this time and to be on the safe side she is given this right of making her application whilst she is still able to get about.

The magistrates may grant a summons upon a bastardy application but never a warrant. If the summons is served and the putative father does not attend the complaint may be heard in his absence.

No order can be made without the evidence of the mother. If she fails to attend at the hearing or dies before she can give her evidence, no order can be made.

The putative father like all defendants in civil actions may be called as a witness for the mother. If he or any other witness refuses to attend he may be compelled to do so by witness summons or warrant as described on page 78.

At the hearing the mother as complainant is, of course, called first. Before she gives evidence of the birth of the child she should be asked if she is single or married; and if married whether she is separated from her husband or not.

Until the Law Reform (Miscellaneous Provisions) Act, 1949, S. 7, was passed, a married woman could give evidence of the paternity of the child only after some other witness or witnesses had proved that her husband had not had access to her at a time when he might have been the father of the child. The law presumes that a child born to a married woman during her marriage is the child of her husband and it would not allow either spouse to give evidence to bastardize it.

The new Act now provides that 'Notwithstanding any rule of law, the evidence of a husband or wife shall be admissible in any proceedings to prove that marital intercourse did or did not take place between them during any period.' No spouse can be compelled to give such evidence.

A married woman cannot apply for a bastardy order whilst she is actually living with her husband nor should proceedings be entertained if it turns out that she has left her husband temporarily in order to obtain an order.

The feature peculiar to bastardy proceedings which distinguishes them from all other civil actions, except those for breach of promise, is that the mother's evidence must be 'corroborated in a material particular' by another witness. If she is unable to produce a second witness or if the witness can give no evidence corroborative of her own, no matter how convinced the justices may be that she is telling the truth and that the defendant is not, they cannot make an order.

What does corroboration amount to? No one has defined it, probably for the good reason that it is indefinable except in broad generalizations of no practical value. Certainly it must be evidence relating to the acts or conduct of the putative father in regard either to the child or to the mother. It would not for example be corroboration to call a witness to support the mother's statement that she had given birth to a child, though this might be a strongly contested issue in bastardy proceedings.

But here is a test which may be suggested. If the proceedings were like other civil complaints would the evidence put forward as corroboration be sufficient to establish a prima facie case if it rested on that alone plus the mother's evidence of the birth of the child and that the defendant was the father? If it is sufficient, it must also be sufficiently corroborative.

The mother's evidence usually consists not only of a statement that she has given birth to a child and that the defendant is the father but also of details of her association with him. Now, suppose the mother's evidence stops short at the mere evidence of birth and an allegation of paternity. Adding to this the evidence of the witness, is there a prima facie case against the defendant?

This sounds somewhat involved but is simple enough in practice. Let us apply it to some of the cases in which the judges have considered what is and what is not corroboration.

The mother gives evidence only of the birth of the child and names the defendant as the father. A witness following her says, 'I accused the defendant of being the father and he made no reply.' But for the insistence of the Act upon corroboration, would not the defendant's silence be sufficient evidence to obtain an order providing always, of course, that the court believed the mother and her witness and disbelieved the man? The judges have held such evidence to be 'corroboration in a material particular' and few will disagree with them.

Again, to take another case, the mother gives evidence of the birth and names the defendant as father as before. The corroborating witness says he saw the couple out courting. Obviously to regard this as sufficient would be as monstrous as to hold upon an action for debt that because a person is seen in a shop he must necessarily have made a purchase.

But on the other hand, if the witness in addition can give evidence of indecent familiarity between the parties during their courtship this may be regarded as corroboration, and in decisions upon the point the judges have so held it to be.

In *Stone* we shall find many of these judicial decisions summarized. In themselves they are an excellent guide to what is corroborative evidence and what is not.

An actual admission of paternity if believed by the court is sufficient corroboration. The provision of accommodation for the mother by the defendant at about the time of the birth may be held to be so too; and the silence of a defendant when taxed with being the father but not generally his failure to answer letters.

Evidence of mere opportunity is not enough. Facial resemblance of the child to the defendant is usually disregarded, but the colour of the child or peculiar racial characteristics might be if it could be shown that the mother had been associating exclusively with a coloured man or, say, a Japanese and the child had a markedly Asiatic appearance.

At some courts the justices refuse to grant a bastardy summons unless the woman is then able to satisfy them that she has evidence corroborative of her story. This is not only wrong but highly prejudicial to the woman. At the hearing the defendant himself may corroborate her by admitting paternity or the woman may call him as a witness to see if having denied his liability hitherto he will persist in his denials upon oath. Or again, she may obtain the evidence between the application and the hearing.

On the other hand, a practice obtaining at many courts of warning the woman that corroboration will be needed and of explaining to her in simple terms what is meant by corroboration has everything to be said for it.

In deciding whether the mother's evidence is corroborated or not, the magistrates do no more than take a preliminary step. In their preoccupation with this step, they must not forget that a still greater question awaits them – which of the parties do they believe? The corroborative evidence may be very strong but, if the courts accept the denials of the defendant, no order can be made. In one instance, for example, the witness said she was present when intercourse took place between the parties on an August Bank holiday – no stronger corroborative evidence could be adduced than this. The defendant, however, was able to prove that on this day he was two hundred miles and more away and had won a race at a well-known meeting.

In deciding between the parties, it must be remembered that the Bastardy Acts set the magistrates upon a quest not of the father of the child, but of the putative father. Theirs is a task not of biological precision but of judicial approximation. 'Putative' means 'commonly reckoned or deemed.' In this sense it cannot be used in the way it generally is – that is to say, the man to whom paternity is attributed by local gossip, but in the sense that the justices, having heard both sides, deem the defendant to be the father, though in fact he may not be at all.

Unlike other civil proceedings, if the mother loses her first application she is entitled to ask for a second summons if later she is able to offer other evidence.

If the court decides to make an order, the maximum sum is thirty shillings per week until the child is sixteen. If the defendant fails to pay, the order may be enforced in the same way as a matrimonial order as explained at page 201.

The magistrates may also order the defendant to pay the expenses incidental to the birth, the funeral expenses if the child has died before the making of the order, and the costs of the proceedings.

On the other hand, a complaint cannot be entertained if the child is stillborn and, of course, the mother can obtain no compensation for any loss she may have sustained before the child is born.

The amount of the weekly sum payable under the order may be varied at the instance of either party by summons, but the finding of paternity cannot be set aside except upon appeal.

Appeal is to Quarter Sessions. The defendant may appeal against the making of an order and the woman against a refusal to make an order. Either too may appeal against the variation of the order.

By the Maintenance Orders Act, 1950, Section 3, a woman residing in England can apply for an affiliation order against a man residing in Scotland or Northern Ireland 'if the Act of intercourse resulting in the birth of the child or any act of intercourse between the parties which may have resulted therein took place in England.'

Such orders may be registered in Scotland or Northern Ireland and enforced by the authorities of those countries.

CHAPTER 39

FINALLY

READERS of this brief outline of the powers and work of the magistrates' courts will put it down with impatience. They will be eager now to turn to the real thing – to Acts of Parliament, to standard text-books, above all to the reported cases.

Which are the best books?

Stone, of course, is as inexhaustible as invaluable. The best books on criminal law are Professor Kenny's *Outlines of Criminal Law* and *Cases on Criminal Law*. Both these books are based on lectures given by Professor Kenny at Cambridge. They are most entertainingly written and are packed with interesting and amusing erudition. Excellent reading too is *Wills on Circumstantial Evidence* recently brought up to date by Mr Vernon Gattie.

There are also a number of text-books on the practice with regard to the more important branches of magisterial law and practice; as, for example, the Juvenile Courts, matrimonial jurisdiction, and affiliation. Many of these can be obtained at the public libraries.

But, however good our collection of books may be, we shall often find ourselves faced with questions to which they give no answer. Times and conditions change, giving rise to new problems upon which there are no authoritative decisions. The magistrates will have to decide them out of hand, in the light of their own native wit.

Tennyson's vision of the law broadening down from precedent to precedent gives the impression of a royal progress assured of its destination and time of arrival, but this is far from being a true picture of the working of our system of case law. It is a thing of fits and starts, over-elaborating some pages of the law and ignoring others.

Let us look a last time, for example, at the problem of the motor-car on the pavement outlined in Chapter 3. It was not decided by the judges until after a quarter of a century of motor-car legislation. Up to 1932 each bench had to solve it in its own way.

A yet more striking example is provided by the Vagrancy Act. Under it a 'suspected person or reputed thief loitering with intent to commit a felony' can be sent to prison for three months. But who is a 'suspected person or reputed thief?' Does it mean anyone whose actions have brought him under suspicion or is the phrase limited to a person who has already been convicted? It was not until the Act had almost attained its centenary that the question was considered by the judges. Yet here is a section under which some thousands have been charged annually ever since 1824.

So much for two points which have been decided. We shall find after a short experience of the summary courts that there are many others which have not been decided at all. When they arise the courts are left to their own devices.

Apart from all this, we must not get into the way of thinking that the law is no more than a collection of 'words, words, words' or that the administration of justice is a craft to be learnt wholly from books. Judges and magistrates are interpreters of their day and generation just as much as priests and poets and statesmen. If they keep their attention too closely upon the records of the past, they may fail to catch the spirit of the present.

'Heaven,' wrote Wordsworth, 'lies about us in our infancy.' He went on to show that in later life its place is taken by more mundane things. The law, we may well believe, is one of them. Just as intangible as the poet's imaginings, it is in the air around us. Events happen and seemingly out of nothing new principles take shape, new rights are formulated.

The part played by the courts in giving these new principles a local habitation and a name is great. With such unpromising material as a leaking reservoir and a snail decomposing in a bottle of ginger beer, puisne judges of the High Court have started new branches of law of the growth of which we have still not seen the last. Less spectacularly the magistrates work in the same way. The law is part of the atmosphere of their courts as much as of any other, no matter how exalted, and the principles and rules which they help to form usually affect a much greater number of our fellow countrymen and much more intimately. Witness the 'single woman' and 'workmen' decisions in Chapters 3 and 38.

Too much learning, too many books sometimes make for pedantry, sometimes for indecision, sometimes, in the striking phrases of Lord Justice du Parcq, for the overvaluation of 'the form of procedure' at the expense of the 'substance of the right'.

The eyes of the bench should be as much as possible upon the living drama continually unfolding before it, alert to note its movement and its colour, its fleeting shades, so revealing and so easily missed.

With Goethe, we may say

'Theory is grey, my friend,
Green is the immortal tree of life.'

List of Principal Indictable Offences
Triable Summarily with the Defendant's Consent

OFFENCE	STATUTE
ACCOUNTS, falsifying.	Falsification of Accounts Act, 1875, s. 1.
AGRICULTURAL CREDITS, obtaining by fraud.	Agricultural Credits Act, 1928, s. 11.
AIDING and ABETTING.	Larceny Act, 1916, s. 35.
	Any offence triable summarily by virtue of the Criminal Justice Act, 1925, Second Schedule. Paragraph 17.
ANIMALS, killing with intent to steal.	Larceny Act, 1916, s. 4.
ARSON of CROPS, setting fire to.	Malicious Damage Act, 1861, s. 16.
ASSAULT occasioning bodily harm.	Offences against the Person Act, 1861, s. 47.
— indecent on child or young person.	Offences against the Person Act, 1861, ss. 52, 62.
ATTEMPTS.	Attempting to commit any offence triable summarily by virtue of the Criminal Justice Act, 1925, Second Schedule, Paragraph 17.
BODILY HARM, wounding or inflicting.	Offences against the Person Act, 1861, s. 20.
CIVIL SERVANT, larceny or embezzlement by.	Larceny Act, 1916, s. 17 (2).
CLERKS, larceny and embezzlement by.	Larceny Act, 1916, s. 17 (1).
COINAGE, exporting counterfeit.	Coinage Offences Act, 1861, s. 8.
— uttering counterfeit gold or silver coin.	Coinage Offences Act, 1861, s. 9.
— uttering, with possession of other false coin, or followed by second uttering.	Coinage Offences Act, 1861, s. 10.
— having three or more pieces of false coin.	Coinage Offences Act, 1861, s. 11.
— uttering foreign coin, etc., as British coin.	Coinage Offences Act, 1861, s. 13.
— uttering base copper coin.	Coinage Offences Act, 1861, s. 15.
— defacing coin.	Coinage Offences Act, 1861, s. 16.
— uttering counterfeit foreign coin.	Coinage Offences Act, 1861, s. 20.

OFFENCE	STATUTE
COINAGE, second offence uttering counterfeit foreign coin.	Coinage Offences Act, 1861, s. 21.
— counterfeit foreign coin other than gold or silver.	Coinage Offences Act, 1861, s. 22.
CONVERSION, FRAUDULENT to the value of £20.	Criminal Justice Act, 1948, 9th Schedule.
CREDIT, obtaining by fraud.	Debtors Act, 1869, s. 13 (1).
CROPS, setting fire to.	Malicious Damage Act, 1861, s. 16.
DAMAGE, destroying or damaging trees, etc.	Malicious Damage Act, 1861, s. 20.
— to property generally.	Malicious Damage Act, 1861, s. 51, as amended by the Criminal Justice Administration Act, 1914, s. 14.
DEMANDING PROPERTY ON FORGED DOCUMENTS.	Forgery Act, 1913, s. 7 (a), as limited by paragraph 10 of the Second Schedule of the Criminal Justice Act, 1925.
DIVERSION OF LETTER, criminal — from addressee.	Post Office Act, 1908, s. 54.
DOCKS, larceny from ships, etc.	Larceny Act, 1916, s. 15 (1).
DOG stealing (after previous conviction summarily).	Larceny Act, 1916, s. 5 (1).
— possession of stolen (after previous conviction summarily).	Larceny Act, 1916, s. 5 (2).
— taking reward for recovering stolen dog.	Larceny Act, 1916, s. 5 (3).
DWELLING-HOUSE, larceny in.	Larceny Act, 1916, s. 13 (a).
ELECTRICITY, abstracting.	Larceny Act, 1916, s. 10.
EMBEZZLEMENT, larceny and, by clerks or servants.	Larceny Act, 1916, s. 17 (1).
— larceny or, by civil servant or police officer.	Larceny Act, 1916, s. 17 (2).
FALSE PRETENCES.	Larceny Act, 1916, s. 32 (1).
FALSIFYING ACCOUNTS.	Falsification of Accounts Act, 1875, s. 1.
FIXTURES, stealing or damaging with intent to steal.	Larceny Act, 1916, s. 8 (1).
FORGERY, valuable security.	Forgery Act, 1913, s. 2 (2) (a), as limited by paragraph 10 of the Second Schedule of the Criminal Justice Act, 1925.

OFFENCE	STATUTE
FORGERY, demanding property on forged documents.	Forgery Act, 1913, s. 7 (a).
— of passport.	Criminal Justice Act, 1925, s. 36 (1).
FRAUDULENT CONVERSION, to value of £20.	Larceny Act, 1916, s. 20.
GOODS IN MANUFACTURE, larceny of.	Larceny Act, 1916, s. 9.
INCITING.	Common Law.
INDECENT ASSAULT, on child or young person under 16.	Offences against the Person Act, ss. 52, 62.
INDECENT PUBLICATIONS, or obscene.	Common Law.
KILLING ANIMALS TO STEAL.	.Larceny Act, 1916, s. 4.
LARCENY, simple.	Larceny Act, 1916, s. 2.
— killing animals with intent.	Larceny Act, 1916, s. 4.
— dog stealing (after previous conviction summarily).	Larceny Act, 1916, s. 5 (1).
— possession of stolen dog.	Larceny Act, 1916, s. 5 (2).
— taking reward for recovering stolen dog.	Larceny Act, 1916, s. 5 (3).
— stealing or damaging fixtures with intent.	Larceny Act, 1916, s. 8 (1).
— stealing or damaging trees with intent.	Larceny Act, 1916, s. 8 (2).
— stealing or damaging plants with intent.	Larceny Act, 1916, s. 8 (3).
— of goods in process of manufacture.	Larceny Act, 1916, s. 9.
— abstracting electricity.	Larceny Act, 1916, s. 10.
— in a dwelling-house.	Larceny Act, 1916, s. 13 (a).
— from person.	Larceny Act, 1916, s. 14.
— from ships, docks, etc.	Larceny Act, 1916, s. 15 (1).
— by tenants or lodgers.	Larceny Act, 1916, s. 16.
— and embezzlement by clerks or servants.	Larceny Act, 1916, s. 17 (1).
— or embezzlement by civil servant or police officer.	Larceny Act, 1916, s. 17 (2).
LETTER, criminal diversion of from addressee.	Post Office Act, 1908, s. 54.
LODGER, larceny by tenants or.	Larceny Act, 1916, s. 16.
MAIL BAG, FRAUDULENT retention of, or postal packet.	Post Office Act, 1908, s. 53.
— receiving, or postal packet.	Post Office Act, 1908, s. 52, and Larceny Act, 1916, s. 33 (2).

OFFENCE	STATUTE
MAIL BAG SENT BY POST OFFICE VESSEL, taking or opening.	Post Office Act, 1908, s. 51.
— stealing.	Post Office Act, 1908, s. 50 (a).
MAIL, stopping to rob or search.	Post Office Act, 1908, s. 50 (d).
NATIONAL HEALTH STAMPS, offences as to.	Stamp Duties Management Act, 1891, s. 13, applied by the National Health Insurance (Stamps) Regulations, 1924.
OBSCENE PUBLICATIONS, indecent.	Common Law.
PASSPORT, forgery of.	Criminal Justice Act, 1925, s. 36 (1).
PERSON, larceny from the.	Larceny Act, 1916, s. 14.
PLANTS, stealing or damaging, with intent to steal.	Larceny Act, 1916, s. 8 (3).
POLICE OFFICER, larceny or embezzlement by.	Larceny Act, 1916, s. 17 (2).
POST OFFICE OFFENCES, stealing mail bag.	Post Office Act, 1908, s. 50 (a).
— stealing postal packet.	Post Office Act, 1908, s. 50 (b).
— stealing from postal packet.	Post Office Act, 1908, s. 50 (c).
— stopping mail to rob or search.	Post Office Act, 1908, s. 50 (d).
— taking or opening mail bag sent by Post Office vessel.	Post Office Act, 1908, s. 51.
— stealing, etc., postal packet by postal employee.	Post Office Act, 1908, s. 55.
— receiving mail bag or postal packet.	Post Office Act, 1908, s. 52.
— fraudulent retention of mail bag or postal packet.	Post Office Act, 1908, s. 53.
— criminal diversion of letter from addressee.	Post Office Act, 1908, s. 54.
— opening or delaying postal packets.	Post Office Act, 1908, s. 56.
RECEIVING mail bag or postal packet.	Post Office Act, 1908, s. 52.
REWARD FOR STOLEN DOG.	Larceny Act, 1916, s. 5 (3).
SERVANTS, larceny and embezzlement by.	Larceny Act, 1916, s. 17 (1).
SHIPS, larceny from.	Larceny Act, 1916, s. 15 (1).
STAMPS, offences as to.	Stamp Duty Management Act, 1891, s. 13.
— offences as to National Health.	Stamp Duty Management Act, 1891, s. 13, applied by the National Health Insurance (Stamps) Regulations, 1924.

OFFENCE	STATUTE
STAMPS, offences as to Unemployment Insurance.	Stamp Duty Management Act, 1891, s. 13, applied by the Unemployment Insurance (Stamps) Regulations, 1924.
STATUTORY DECLARATIONS, false.	Perjury Act, 1911, s. 5 (a).
SUICIDE, attempting.	Common Law.
TELEGRAPHIC MESSAGES, disclosing or intercepting.	Telegraph Act, 1868, s. 20.
TENANT, larceny by.	Larceny Act, 1916, s. 16.
TREES, destroying or damaging.	Malicious Damage Act, 1861, s. 20.
— stealing or damaging with intent to steal.	Larceny Act, 1916, s. 8 (2).
UNEMPLOYMENT STAMPS, offences as to.	Stamp Duties Management Act, 1891, s. 13, applied by the Unemployment Insurance (Stamps) Regulations, 1924.
VALUABLE SECURITY, destroying etc.	Larceny Act, 1861, s. 27.
— forging.	Forgery Act, 1913, s. 2 (2) (a), as limited by the Criminal Justice Act, 1925, Second Schedule, Paragraph 10.
WILFUL DAMAGE, destroying trees.	Malicious Damage Act, 1861, s. 20.
— to property generally.	Malicious Damage Act, 1861, s. 51, as amended by the Criminal Justice Administration Act, 1914 s. 14.
WOUNDING, or inflicting bodily harm.	Offences against the Person Act, 1861, s. 20.

Principal Summary Offences for which the Defendant may Claim to be Tried by a Jury

OFFENCE	STATUTE
Aiding deserters.	Army Act, 1881, s. 153.
Buying regimental necessities.	Army Act, 1881, s. 156.
Various offences.	Bankruptcy Act, 1914.
Keeping betting house.	Betting Act, 1853, s. 3.
Ill treatment or neglect.	Children and Young Persons Act, 1933, s. 1.
Various offences.	Companies Act, 1929.
Keeping or managing brothel (second offence).	Criminal Law Amendment Act, 1885, s. 13.
Offences against the Act.	Dangerous Drugs Act, 1920, s. 13 (2).
Master neglecting to find food, clothing, etc., for apprentice.	Employers and Workmen Act, 1875, s. 6.
Keeping or using Gaming House.	Gaming Act, 1845, s. 4.
	Gaming Act, 1854, s. 4.
Stealing beast or bird.	Larceny Act, 1861, s. 21.
Stealing dog.	Larceny Act, 1861, s. 18.
Stealing plants, roots, fruit, etc., growing in gardens.	Larceny Act, 1861, s. 36.
Damage to plants, roots, fruit, etc., growing in garden or orchard.	Malicious Damage Act, 1861, s. 23.
Killing or wounding dog, bird, or beast (not cattle).	Malicious Damage Act, 1861, s. 41.
Forging or falsely applying trade mark, or other offences.	Merchandise Marks Act, 1887, s. 2.
Bringing spirits or tobacco into.	Prison Act, 1865, s. 38.
Driving when disqualified.	Road Traffic Act, 1930, s. 7 (4).
Reckless or Dangerous driving.	Road Traffic Act, 1930, s. 11.
Driving when under influence of drink or drugs.	Road Traffic Act, 1930, s. 15.
Forgery of licences and certificates.	Road Traffic Act, 1930, 112.

INDEX

HOW MONEY IS MANAGED

Paul Einzig

A312

This book describes the manifold ends of monetary policy, and the even wider variety of means which may be employed in pursuing those ends. The author gives an account of the remarkable changes that have taken place in our time in the objectives followed by governments in their monetary policy, and also in the methods employed by them.

The subject of the book is of interest not only to the specialist, but also to the layman who wishes to understand the 'why' and 'how' of government action in the monetary sphere. Such action should be of interest to everybody, because it is liable to affect his welfare. Why do the authorities sometimes wish to encourage a rise in prices and at other times a fall? What was the object of the suspension of the gold standard in 1931 or of the devaluation of the pound in 1939? Why were interest rates kept low for nearly twenty years, and why were they raised in 1951–2? These are some of the questions answered in this book in a simple language, understandable to the average reader of newspapers.   (2s 6d)

ALSO AVAILABLE

ECONOMICS OF EVERYDAY LIFE (A221)

Gertrude Williams (2s)